A *Gift* for You

As a way of saying thank you for purchasing this journal, we hope you'll check out the free companion website where you'll find a collection of printable mindfulness checklists, affirmation worksheets, and bonus videos.

Go to this page for access to the website.
mindfulz.com

About the Authors

Steve Scott is a bestselling author of numerous books where he provides daily action plans for every area of your life: mindfulness, health, fitness, work and personal relationships. Unlike other personal development guides, his content focuses on taking action. Instead of reading over-hyped strategies that rarely work in the real world, you'll get information that can be immediately implemented.

Barrie Davenport is a certified personal coach, thought leader, best selling author, and founder of the award winning personal development site Live Bold and Bloom where she offers practical strategies for living happier, more successful, and more mindful lives.

Together Steve and Barrie have published four books, including:
Declutter Your Mind: How to Stop Worrying, Relieve Anxiety, and Eliminate Negative Thinking and *10-Minute Mindfulness: 71 Habits for Living in the Present Moment.*

Why Mindfulness?

> *"Mindfulness is the aware, balanced acceptance of the present experience. It isn't more complicated than that. It is opening to or receiving the present moment, pleasant or unpleasant, just as it is, without either clinging to it or rejecting it."*

Sylvia Boorstein

The concept of mindfulness is very simple.

When you are mindful, you are intentionally aware of the present moment. You consciously direct your awareness to whatever you are doing, thinking, or observing.

Making tea.

Looking out the window.

Having a conversation.

Folding laundry.

Working on a project.

Exercising.

Journaling.

In addition to being purposefully aware, there is another element of mindfulness—the practice of non-judgment.

Non-judgment means you observe your experiences, thoughts, and feelings from a distance, without labeling them as good or bad, right or wrong. This detachment from judging the moment but simply experiencing it removes the filter of appraisal, which pulls us away from the actual experience.

Left to its own devices, the brain automatically judges things as right or wrong, good or bad, useful or not useful, and so on. This judgment occurs so quickly that our moments are tainted by our thoughts about them before we can fully process the experience.

Adding *non-judgmental awareness* to your mindfulness practice helps remove these filters so you can fully and authentically experience the moment. In addition, our judgments about our thoughts often cause us unnecessary anxiety. Avoiding this suffering is another compelling reason to leave judgments by the wayside.

At first, it will be hard to be a detached observer of your experiences, and simply experience them. But the more you practice mindfulness in daily life, the more adept you become at living purely in the now.

You might wonder why you should bother with this practice at all. Why do you need mindfulness in your life?

As we say in our book, *10-Minute Mindfulness*, "For those who are frequently pulled away by the usual preoccupations of daily living (and isn't that most of us?), mindfulness affords a richer appreciation of the moment and a larger perspective on life. It also helps us alter our habitual responses by pausing long enough to choose how we act."

Being more intentional in our choices is reason enough to embrace mindfulness habits. But science has confirmed there are many additional physical and emotional benefits. Mindfulness practices have been researched extensively, and shown to:

- Reduce rumination and overthinking.

- Decrease stress by lowering levels of the stress hormone cortisol.

- Improve memory, concentration, and performance.

- Help maintain emotional stability.

- Improve relationship happiness.

- Reduce symptoms of anxiety and depression.

- Improve sleep.

- Protect against mental illness.

- Provide pain relief.

With the repetition of mindfulness activities, you will create real changes in your brain function and structure. Just as exercise habits will change your body, mindfulness habits will literally reshape your mind.

PRACTICING
Mindfulness Daily

"In this moment, there is plenty of time.
In this moment, you are precisely as you should be.
In this moment, there is infinite possibility."

Victoria Moran

The skills involved in mindfulness aren't brain surgery, but the practice itself is harder than you might think. The ability to incorporate mindfulness into our daily lives is something that requires daily awareness. You first have to remember to do it, and then you need to create strategies for incorporating this practice into your daily routine.

That's where this journal comes in.

The practice of journaling is an excellent mindfulness practice itself, because you are encouraging your mind to be present with your writing. It forces your brain to slow down to better organize your thoughts and consider the big picture.

With *The Mindfulness Journal*, you'll get a double dose of daily mindfulness—through the mindfulness activity outlined in the daily prompts, as well as your time spent journaling about the activity.

Writing about your experiences with mindfulness will help you master the practice, reflect on your thoughts and experiences, and provide a permanent record of your efforts at deepening the amount of purposeful intention in your life.

Most of the mindfulness practices we provide take very little time—most require 10 minutes of effort on your part. Then you will spend a few minutes writing about your experience with the practice. Sometimes you may only write a few sentences. Other times you'll be inspired or invited to write more.

You will need to set aside time during your day to both work on the mindfulness practice and journal about it.

The Mindfulness Journal

"There is something about journal writing that causes us to meditate, to recommit, and to receive spiritual impressions in the process of such pondering."

L. Edward Brown

This journal provides a total of 365 daily writing prompts divided into 52 weekly mindfulness topics. This arrangement gives you seven days to immerse yourself in each topic. It is designed to awaken you to mindfulness in various natural moments throughout your day, as well as with some activities that may be new for you.

This will be a process of self-discovery as you try various ways to practice mindfulness and write about your experiences. It will help you discover what specific activities work best for you and your lifestyle. We invite you to keep your mind and heart open, even if some of the practices seem strange or simplistic. There is a purpose behind each topic, activity, and related prompt.

The practices presented in some of the writing prompts require little more than thought and reflection. Others require performing a specific action or series of actions, either in the moment or during your day. Some journal topics are more suited to morning action and writing, while others are better for evening or right before you go to bed.

For this reason, we suggest you read through the weekly topic and related journal prompts before you begin each week. This will help determine the best time of day to practice the mindfulness habits, and when to write about them.

We encourage you to journal about your mindfulness habit as soon as possible after you practice it, so that your feelings and reactions are fresh on your mind. Because you will be practicing and writing at different times during the day, you may find it harder to stick to your journaling habit if you need a regular routine.

You may find you need to commit to a specific time that is consistent day after day to work through this journal. If this is the case for you, skip any weeks that require you to change your journaling time, and save them for later when you have more fully established the habit of working on this journal.

You don't need to follow the weekly order of topics the way they are presented here. You can move from Week 1 to Week 32, then back to Week 5 if you wish, depending on what you wish to focus on. It is helpful to work the full seven days of topic-related activities so you can delve into each topic. But it is also fine if you want to randomly choose a different prompt from a different topic every day. This is your journal, after all, so use it in the way that feels best for you and your goals.

"A blank page is no empty space. It is brimming with potential... It is a masterpiece in waiting—yours."

A.A. Patawaran

Daily Gratitude

"When you arise in the morning, think of what a precious privilege it is to be alive— to breathe, to think, to enjoy, to love."

Marcus Aurelius

Buddhist monks start the day with chants of gratitude for their blessings. Native American elders begin their ceremonies with prayers of gratitude to mother earth and father sky, to the four directions, to the animal, plant, and mineral brothers and sisters who share our earth and support our life. Tibetan monks and nuns offer prayers of gratitude for the suffering they have been given, saying, "Grant that I might have enough suffering to awaken in the deepest possible compassion and wisdom."

Gratitude is a mindfulness practice that opens you to joy, compassion, and appreciation of the life that sustains you. Begin your morning with awareness that you have awakened to a new day, a blank page full of promise and potential. Before you begin your morning routine, take a deep breath, close your eyes, and focus on all you are grateful for in your life based on the daily prompt.

Best time to journal: *morning*

Day 1

I reflect on the people in my life who have made me feel loved and supported. I feel grateful for...

_____

_____

_____

_____

_____

_____

_____

_____

_____

_____

_____

Day 2

I am mindful of the strengths, skills, and aptitudes I possess that have helped me become who I am. I feel grateful for...

_____

_____

_____

_____

_____

_____

_____

_____

_____

_____

Day 3

I remember all the mentors who have shown me the way and inspired me. I feel grateful for...

_____

_____

_____

_____

_____

_____

_____

_____

_____

_____

_____

Day 4

I am mindful of the home I live in and how it provides a safe and peaceful haven for me and my family. I feel grateful for...

_____

_____

_____

_____

_____

_____

_____

_____

_____

_____

Day 5

I consider the work I do in a career or at home, and how it impacts my life and well-being. I feel grateful for...

_____

_____

_____

_____

_____

_____

_____

_____

_____

_____

_____

Day 6

I am mindful of the beauty of nature, of all living creatures, and the world around me. I feel grateful for...

_____

_____

_____

_____

_____

_____

_____

_____

_____

_____

Day 7

I reflect on all of the lessons I have learned in life so far, and how they have helped me grow and evolve. I feel grateful for...

WEEK 2
Body Awareness

"Attention to the human body brings healing and regeneration. Through awareness of the body we remember who we really are."

Jack Kornfield

Most mindfulness practices begin with your body by drawing your attention to your breath and the quality of sensation. In ancient Buddhist teachings of "The Four Foundations of Mindfulness," the first teaching is "mindfulness of the body," which involves becoming familiar with and even loving the body. Body mindfulness anchors you in the here and now.

Your body can reveal so much about your inner world if you pay attention to it. Every tight muscle, aching joint, and anxious breath gives you a clue to the worries and challenges you carry inside of you. Through body awareness, you have the power to release both the physical and mental distress, as you breathe relaxation and healing into each part of your body.

Best time to journal: *anytime*

Day 1

I visualize a bright and healing beam of light flowing down from the sky, through the top of my head, filling my body with energy and grounding me to the earth. My body responds by...

_____

_____

_____

_____

_____

_____

_____

_____

_____

_____

_____

Day 2

I scan my body for any aches, pains, or tension. I notice these feelings and how I might be resisting them. What are these aches and pains telling me about any mental distress or behavior changes I need to make? What mental resistance to these feelings do I need to drop?

_____

_____

_____

_____

_____

_____

_____

_____

_____

_____

Day 3

I am mindful of the ways my body causes me shame, embarrassment, or unhappiness. How often do I focus on what I hate about my body? How can I show my body more compassion? Today I will write a letter of love and gratitude to my body.

_____

_____

_____

_____

_____

_____

_____

_____

_____

_____

_____

Day 4

As I sit quietly, I notice each breath I take, following the intake of air through my nose and into my lungs, and the slow exhalation as I release the air through my nose. As I repeat this mindful breathing for several minutes, I notice my body...

Day 5

I take a few deep breaths and focus attention on my energy level in my body. Do I feel tired, restless, sleepy, or depleted, or am I energized and invigorated? My energy level is telling me...

_____

_____

_____

_____

_____

_____

_____

_____

_____

_____

Day 6

I focus on all of the organs, muscles, and bones in my body and what their purpose is for my health, sustenance, movement, and sensations. As I focus my attention on these parts of my body, I feel...

_____

_____

_____

_____

_____

_____

_____

_____

_____

_____

_____

Day 7

I sit quietly, take a few deep and cleansing breaths, and perform a relaxation body scan. Starting at my toes, I focus attention on each part of my body, breathing relaxation into each area. I move from my toes upward, relaxing each body part until I reach the top of my head. My body responds by...

_____

_____

_____

_____

_____

_____

_____

_____

_____

_____

_____

WEEK 3

Noticing Thoughts

> *"We are shaped by our thoughts; we become what we think. When the mind is pure, joy follows like a shadow that never leaves."*
>
> Buddha

Your own thoughts can trigger anxiety, unhappiness, and anger, which can keep your mind trapped in a constant negative loop.

This cycle happens because we are unconscious of our thoughts, and allow them to run rampant in our brains without challenging them. Rumination becomes a bad habit—almost an addiction—that leads to suffering and undermines the quality of our lives.

You can change this cycle of suffering by adopting a very simple new habit—observation. By becoming the silent and dispassionate watcher of your thoughts, you understand how unsubstantial your thoughts are, and can release the emotional power they have over you.

Best time to journal: *late afternoon or evening*

Day 1

What is the general nature of my thinking patterns? Do I find myself frequently ruminating, worrying, and focusing on negativity? Does it feel like my thoughts control me?

_____

_____

_____

_____

_____

_____

_____

_____

_____

_____

_____

Day 2

What do my thoughts tell me about me, my reality, and where I focus my mental energy? How do my thoughts affect my daily life?

_____

_____

_____

_____

_____

_____

_____

_____

_____

_____

_____

_____

Day 3

How do my thoughts influence my emotions? What correlations do I see between my thinking patterns and my moods?

_____

_____

_____

_____

_____

_____

_____

_____

_____

_____

_____

Day 4

Today I sit quietly for a few moments and observe my thoughts as they float by in my mind. I don't judge them, I just watch and notice. What does observation reveal to me about my thoughts?

_____

_____

_____

_____

_____

_____

_____

_____

_____

_____

_____

Day 5

As I observe and notice my thoughts as they float by, I wait for a moment of emptiness and space between thoughts. I try to extend this moment of emptiness by pausing thoughts. What do I notice, and how do I feel in these moments of mental space?

_____

_____

_____

_____

_____

_____

_____

_____

_____

_____

_____

Day 6

Today I practice noticing my thoughts throughout the day. I wear a physical reminder (like a rubber band on my wrist) to help me stop and notice my thoughts. What do I need to work on changing about my thoughts?

_____

_____

_____

_____

_____

_____

_____

_____

_____

_____

_____

Day 7

Today I practice noticing my thoughts again, but this time I stop negative thinking to divert my focus to more positive thoughts or actions. What do I notice in my efforts to redirect my thoughts?

_____

_____

_____

_____

_____

_____

_____

_____

_____

_____

_____

WEEK 4
Daily Routine

"Live the actual moment.
Only this actual moment is life."

Thích Nhất Hạnh

The opportunity for mindfulness is in everything you do, in every task and seemingly unimportant activity of your day. Even the most enlightened practitioners are faced with the day-to-day tasks of living, and must translate the freedom of mindfulness into real life.

When you align your attention and mental focus to whatever you are doing, you are truly living. You aren't regretting the past or longing for something in the future. You are here, now, experiencing the beauty and perfection of the moment. This week, your focus will be on your daily routine and bringing mindfulness to your moments throughout each day.

Best time to journal: *various times of day*

Day 1

This morning I awaken and pay full attention to my morning activities. My mind is not elsewhere, thinking about the day ahead. It is here, now, fully engaged in my physical preparations for the day. This is what I noticed...

_____

_____

_____

_____

_____

_____

_____

_____

_____

_____

_____

Day 2

Today in my car, I practice mindful driving. I turn off my phone and the radio. I pay attention to every aspect of driving I normally perform automatically. I am mindful of the ease of travel that driving provides. This is what I noticed...

_____

_____

_____

_____

_____

_____

_____

_____

_____

_____

_____

Day 3

When I encounter a service person today—at the store, post office, a restaurant, or anywhere else—I am mindful of the ways they serve and help me. I notice the real person behind the server and engage with them. This is what I noticed...

_____

_____

_____

_____

_____

_____

_____

_____

_____

_____

_____

Day 4

As I walk from one place to another today, instead of rushing to my destination, I take time to really see my environment and look for things I've never notice before. This is what I noticed...

_____

_____

_____

_____

_____

_____

_____

_____

_____

_____

_____

Day 5

During my work day, I choose a task to give my full and focused attention to. I don't rush through it or allow interruptions or distractions to pull me away. This is what I noticed...

_____

_____

_____

_____

_____

_____

_____

_____

_____

_____

Day 6

At home, I choose a routine chore (like washing dishes or folding clothes) and give my full and focused attention to every element of the chore. This is what I noticed...

_____

_____

_____

_____

_____

_____

_____

_____

_____

_____

_____

Day 7

Tonight, as I prepare for bed, I pay attention to my routine and how it readies me for comfort, coziness, and a good night's sleep.
This is what I noticed...

_____

_____

_____

_____

_____

_____

_____

_____

_____

_____

_____

_____

_____

WEEK 5

10-Minute Meditation

"Meditation is the discovery that the point of life is always arrived at in the immediate moment."

Alan Watts

Meditation is the centerpiece of a mindfulness practice, allowing you to cultivate an attitude of compassionate indifference to your thoughts by ceasing to identify with them. As you strengthen your meditation practice, your thoughts lose their power over you, freeing you to experience deeper levels of joy and self-awareness. During meditation, you observe the patterns of your mind and learn to tame the incessant chattering of your thoughts.

This week, you will focus on a short, 10-minute meditation practice using the journal prompts. Begin each meditation session by sitting comfortably either in a chair or cross-legged on the floor with a cushion. Close your eyes and take a few deep, cleansing breaths.

Gradually become aware of your breathing, and allow your attention to rest in the sensation of breathing. When your thoughts wander, gently let them go and return to the sensation of breathing. Don't judge yourself or your intrusive thoughts. Just lead your mind back to focused attention on breathing.

Best time to journal: *morning or evening*

Day 1

As I meditate today, I simply notice. I notice my intrusive thoughts. I notice sounds. I notice the way my body feels, and any pain or discomfort. In meditation today, I discovered...

_____

_____

_____

_____

_____

_____

_____

_____

_____

_____

_____

Day 2

In my meditation today, I focus on self-compassion. I visualize myself as my own loving parent or compassionate friend who holds me tenderly and shows me unconditional love.
In meditation today, I discovered...

_____

_____

_____

_____

_____

_____

_____

_____

_____

_____

Day 3

*Today's meditation focuses on compassion for someone I love.
I visualize my loved one and my heartfelt desire that
he or she feels safe, loved, and supported.
In meditation today, I discovered...*

_____

_____

_____

_____

_____

_____

_____

_____

_____

_____

Day 4

As I meditate today, I ponder the uncertainty of life and how I can't know what the future will bring. I lean into that uncertainty and rest in it with calm openness and acceptance.
In meditation today, I discovered...

_____

_____

_____

_____

_____

_____

_____

_____

_____

_____

_____

Day 5

Today in meditation I consider a conflict I have with someone, and imagine bringing the highest possible intentions and compassion to my next encounter with this person.
In meditation today, I discovered...

_____

_____

_____

_____

_____

_____

_____

_____

_____

_____

_____

_____

Day 6

As I meditate today, I notice my emotions and moods. As emotions and feelings arise, I simply name them without judgment. "This is anxiety." "This is sleepiness." In meditation today, I discovered...

_____

_____

_____

_____

_____

_____

_____

_____

_____

_____

_____

Day 7

Today in meditation I notice the pains and discomforts in my body. I do not resist them, but rather breathe into them and hold them with care and love. In meditation today, I discovered...

_____

_____

_____

_____

_____

_____

_____

_____

_____

_____

_____

_____

WEEK 6

Inspirational Reading

"Inspiration is the greatest gift because it opens your life to many new possibilities. Each day becomes more meaningful, and your life is enhanced when your actions are guided by what inspires you."

Bernie Siegel

Rather than beginning your day with information overload from your smartphone or TV, you can choose to read inspiring books or articles. An important part of being a mindful person includes being intentional about what you feed your mind, as well as challenging your own beliefs and assumptions by reading about the perspectives of others.

This requires an intentional decision to read books that uplift, educate, and support your values and goals. Prepare for this week's mindfulness work by choosing a spiritual reading, a book of daily quotations, or a personal growth book that encourages or motivates you.

You might select a biography of someone you find inspirational, or a novel that stokes your curiosity. Spend five minutes each day reading, and then write about what you have learned or discovered.

Best time to journal: *morning or evening*

Day 1

My reading topic today inspired, motivated, enlightened, or challenged me in the following ways...

Day 2

*My reading topic today inspired, motivated, enlightened,
or challenged me in the following ways...*

_____

_____

_____

_____

_____

_____

_____

_____

_____

_____

_____

Day 3

*My reading topic today inspired, motivated, enlightened,
or challenged me in the following ways...*

_____

_____

_____

_____

_____

_____

_____

_____

_____

_____

_____

_____

_____

_____

Day 4

My reading topic today inspired, motivated, enlightened, or challenged me in the following ways...

_____

_____

_____

_____

_____

_____

_____

_____

_____

_____

_____

_____

Day 5

My reading topic today inspired, motivated, enlightened, or challenged me in the following ways...

_____

_____

_____

_____

_____

_____

_____

_____

_____

_____

_____

_____

_____

Day 6

*My reading topic today inspired, motivated, enlightened,
or challenged me in the following ways...*

_____

_____

_____

_____

_____

_____

_____

_____

_____

_____

_____

Day 7

*My reading topic today inspired, motivated, enlightened,
or challenged me in the following ways...*

_____

_____

_____

_____

_____

_____

_____

_____

_____

_____

_____

_____

_____

Set a Daily Intention

"You are what your deepest desire is. As your desire is, so is your intention. As your intention is, so is your will. As your will is, so is your deed. As your deed is, so is your destiny."

Hindu text, the Upanishads

Intention implies determination, will, and resolve. When you set a daily intention, you resolve to make it happen. There's a boldness to an intention in which you are determined to prioritize an action to the exclusion of other activities.

Intentions give you a sense of purpose, as well as the motivation to achieve your purpose. An intention is the fuel behind all your dreams and goals, the ones that are most valuable and important to you. By setting a daily intention, you laser-focus on your deepest desires and what you will do today to bring them to fruition.

Your job with a daily intention is to plant it into the depths of your consciousness by writing about it and then speaking your intention out loud with a phrase like, "I intend to let inner peace be my guide today with all of my decisions" or "I intend to finish my project today." Use the daily prompts to help you with a specific focus for your intention.

Best time to journal: *morning*

Day 1

Today I focus my intention on a goal or outcome I want to achieve.
My intention is...

_____

_____

_____

_____

_____

_____

_____

_____

_____

_____

_____

Day 2

Today I focus my intention on my relationship with my love partner or spouse. My intention is...

_____

_____

_____

_____

_____

_____

_____

_____

_____

_____

_____

Day 3

Today I focus my intention on my relationship with someone else I am close to. My intention is...

_____

_____

_____

_____

_____

_____

_____

_____

_____

_____

_____

Day 4

Today I focus my intention on my mental or emotional state.
My intention is...

_____

_____

_____

_____

_____

_____

_____

_____

_____

_____

_____

Day 5

Today I focus my intention on my spiritual life or personal growth.
My intention is...

_____

_____

_____

_____

_____

_____

_____

_____

_____

_____

_____

Day 6

Today I focus my intention on creativity.
My intention is...

_____

_____

_____

_____

_____

_____

_____

_____

_____

_____

_____

Day 7

Today I focus my attention on _____.
My intention is...

_____

_____

_____

_____

_____

_____

_____

_____

_____

_____

_____

_____

_____

WEEK 8
Set Three Goals

> *"Indeed, your ability to focus on this and suppress that is the key to controlling your experience and, ultimately, your well-being."*

Winifred Gallagher

This week, you'll define three important activities you want to achieve for the day, and determine a way to get them done.

Why three goals? Because three is a manageable number. Rather than writing a to-do list of many items, narrow your list to the three that you know with certainty you can achieve during the day. You can always do more, as long as you achieve your top three.

Having just three goals also allows you the time and mental energy to focus on them thoroughly, without pressure to rush through each action in order to get to the next one. Taking your time with each goal allows you to enjoy the process of completing them.

Spending a few minutes to set and write down your goals for the day allows you to be more creative, proactive, and thoughtful about how you structure your day and what you accomplish.

Best time to journal: *morning*

Day 1

*These are my three goals for today and
how I intend to achieve them.*

_____

_____

_____

_____

_____

_____

_____

_____

_____

_____

_____

Day 2

*These are my three goals for today and
how I intend to achieve them.*

_____

_____

_____

_____

_____

_____

_____

_____

_____

_____

_____

Day 3

*These are my three goals for today and
how I intend to achieve them.*

_____

_____

_____

_____

_____

_____

_____

_____

_____

_____

_____

_____

_____

Day 4

*These are my three goals for today and
how I intend to achieve them.*

_____

_____

_____

_____

_____

_____

_____

_____

_____

_____

_____

_____

Day 5

These are my three goals for today and how I intend to achieve them.

_____

_____

_____

_____

_____

_____

_____

_____

_____

_____

_____

Day 6

These are my three goals for today and how I intend to achieve them.

_____

_____

_____

_____

_____

_____

_____

_____

_____

_____

_____

Day 7

*These are my three goals for today and
how I intend to achieve them.*

Visualize Your Day

> *"Formulate and stamp indelibly on your mind a mental picture of yourself as succeeding. Hold this picture tenaciously and never permit it to fade. Your mind will seek to develop this picture!"*

Dr. Norman Vincent Peale

Visualization is a mindfulness tool using mental imagery to help you mentally rehearse an outcome or bring about a state of relaxation. The act of visualizing requires focus and frees the mind from mental chatter and negativity. It can be used in daily life to relieve stress, enhance motivation, and add more power to your physical and mental efforts.

This week, you will practice a daily visualization exercise to support your efforts with goals and desired outcomes. Sit comfortably and take a few deep breaths to quiet your mind and get into a more meditative state. Then mentally picture a blank slate. From that blank slate, begin your visualization.

As you visualize, picture yourself reaching the goal or outcome first, as if it were a movie and you were the lead character. Then picture all of the steps involved— exactly what you are doing, how you look, who is around you, where you are, and how you feel. Get as specific and detailed as possible. Then write about your visualization to reinforce your imagery.

Best time to journal: *morning*

Day 1

*Today I visualize the following outcome and the specific actions
I'll take to reach that outcome.*

_____

_____

_____

_____

_____

_____

_____

_____

_____

_____

_____

Day 2

*Today I visualize the following outcome and the specific actions
I'll take to reach that outcome.*

_____

_____

_____

_____

_____

_____

_____

_____

_____

_____

_____

Day 3

*Today I visualize the following outcome and the specific actions
I'll take to reach that outcome.*

_____

_____

_____

_____

_____

_____

_____

_____

_____

_____

_____

Day 4

Today I visualize the following outcome and the specific actions I'll take to reach that outcome.

_____

_____

_____

_____

_____

_____

_____

_____

_____

_____

_____

Day 5

Today I visualize the following outcome and the specific actions I'll take to reach that outcome.

_____

_____

_____

_____

_____

_____

_____

_____

_____

_____

_____

_____

Day 6

*Today I visualize the following outcome and the specific actions
I'll take to reach that outcome.*

_____

_____

_____

_____

_____

_____

_____

_____

_____

_____

_____

Day 7

*Today I visualize the following outcome and the specific actions
I'll take to reach that outcome.*

_____

_____

_____

_____

_____

_____

_____

_____

_____

_____

_____

_____

_____

WEEK 10

Creating Daily Rituals

"The more you praise and celebrate your life, the more there is in life to celebrate."

Oprah Winfrey

Rituals are actions we imbue with meaning and significance that enhance our lives in some way. They are performed in a prescribed way that lends an element of sacredness to the occasion, and they slow us down enough that we can connect to the present moment.

Rituals provide structure in our otherwise random lives, and they foster deeper connections with the people we love. They help us celebrate our values in a meaningful way, solidify commitments, and reinforce beliefs. And they inspire us to feel gratitude for the occasions they are built around.

When you ritualize simple daily activities, they transform from unconscious habits to meaningful moments of joy, significance, and celebration. This week, you will focus on creating rituals around an existing activity. You can design your ritual by preparing your environment, outlining actions, choosing the best time, including others, and using prescribed gestures or words.

Best time to journal: *various times of day*

Day 1

Today I create a ritual around writing in this journal. Here is how I celebrated my journal writing time, and how it made me feel...

_____

_____

_____

_____

_____

_____

_____

_____

_____

_____

_____

Day 2

This morning I create a ritual around my morning cup tea or coffee by paying full attention to all aspects of preparation, drinking, savoring, and cleaning up. This is how I celebrated my morning beverage, and how it made me feel...

_____

_____

_____

_____

_____

_____

_____

_____

_____

_____

Day 3

Today I create a ritual around making my bed slowly, mindfully, and with attention to each step of the process. This is how I ritualized this task, and how it made me feel...

_____

_____

_____

_____

_____

_____

_____

_____

_____

_____

_____

_____

_____

Day 4

Today I create a ritual around decluttering and organizing a small space, like my desk or a cluttered area at home. This is how I ritualized this task, and how it made me feel...

_____

_____

_____

_____

_____

_____

_____

_____

_____

_____

_____

Day 5

Today I create a ritual around reading something motivating or inspirational. This is how I celebrated this reading time, and how it made me feel...

_____

_____

_____

_____

_____

_____

_____

_____

_____

_____

_____

_____

Day 6

*This evening I create a ritual around preparing for bed. This is how
I made this time more special and meaningful, and
how it made me feel...*

_____

_____

_____

_____

_____

_____

_____

_____

_____

_____

_____

Day 7

Today I choose my own activity to ritualize, or I create a brand new ritual. This is how I celebrated this ritual, and how it made me feel...

_____

_____

_____

_____

_____

_____

_____

_____

_____

_____

_____

_____

WEEK 11

Mindful Eating

"Mindful eating replaces self-criticism with self-nurturing. It replaces shame with respect for your own inner wisdom."

Jan Chozen Bays

For many people, meals are often a grab-and-go event, consumed quickly and mindlessly. In our modern lives, there is little time to prepare, savor, and appreciate what we are eating. We become disconnected from our source of sustenance and energy.

Preparing food and eating it more mindfully not only allows you to be present with the experience, but also can help you prevent overeating, lose weight, and become more aware of your body's needs.

You may not have the time to be mindful about your meals every day, but you can take this week to pay more attention to your eating habits, and how mindfulness around eating impacts your experience of food and your body's need for nourishment.

Best time to journal: *various times of day*

Day 1

Today I am mindful of my body sending me signals of hunger, and I only eat when I feel hungry. I avoid eating mindlessly when bored, or to soothe myself. This is what I noticed about listening to my body's need for food...

_____

_____

_____

_____

_____

_____

_____

_____

_____

_____

_____

Day 2

Today I focus on thoughtfully planning a meal. I think carefully about my food choices, the ingredients I'll need, and what is involved in preparing the food. With this exercise, I noticed...

_____

_____

_____

_____

_____

_____

_____

_____

_____

_____

Day 3

I am fully attentive to preparing food for my meal. I wash and chop fruits and veggies with care. I season, stir, sauté, and blend, noticing the changes in the food, the aromas, and the sounds of the food cooking. This is what I noticed during this food preparation time...

_____

_____

_____

_____

_____

_____

_____

_____

_____

_____

_____

_____

Day 4

My focus today is creating the environment for a mindful meal, whether with my family or alone, by creating a ritual around the dining experience and making it special. This is what I noticed about making the meal a ritualized experience...

_____

_____

_____

_____

_____

_____

_____

_____

_____

_____

_____

_____

Day 5

Before I eat a meal that I or someone else has prepared, I take time today to notice the food, smell the aromas, and feel gratitude for the bounty before me. Taking this moment made me feel...

Day 6

Today, as I eat my meals, I eat and chew more slowly than usual, paying mindful attention to every bite, noticing the various flavors as the food moves around my tongue. I make each bite a micro-mindfulness experience. This is what I noticed as I savored my food today...

_____

_____

_____

_____

_____

_____

_____

_____

_____

_____

Day 7

Today I focus my attention on noticing when I am full during meals. I stop eating when I notice I am satiated. This is what I noticed when I paid attention to my fullness...

_____

_____

_____

_____

_____

_____

_____

_____

_____

_____

_____

_____

_____

Practicing Presence

"When you love someone, the best thing you can offer is your presence. How can you love if you are not there?"

Thích Nhất Hạnh

How many families around the world begin their days with little to no interaction with the people they hold most dear? They rush to and from work, school, and other activities. When at home, they are distracted by technology and television. What are we working so hard for, anyway, if not to spend quality time with our loved ones? How can we have close relationships if we aren't fully present for those we love?

Being present with someone means you are fully attentive, engaged, and focused on the other person. You aren't looking at your phone, distracted by the television, or thinking about the next thing you need to do. You are actively listening, responding, and showing with your words, expressions, and demeanor that you are completely in the moment with this person.

This week you will focus on being present with those who are closest to you—your spouse, partner, children, parents, and friends.

Best time to journal: *evening or before bed*

Day 1

I spent time today being fully present and engaged with _____.
This is how I spent my time with him/her, and how
this time together made me feel...

_____

_____

_____

_____

_____

_____

_____

_____

_____

_____

_____

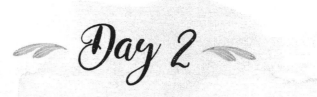

Day 2

I spent time today being fully present and engaged with _____.
This is how I spent my time with him/her, and how
this time together made me feel...

_____

_____

_____

_____

_____

_____

_____

_____

_____

_____

_____

Day 3

I spent time today being fully present and engaged with _____.
This is how I spent my time with him/her, and how
this time together made me feel...

_____

_____

_____

_____

_____

_____

_____

_____

_____

_____

_____

_____

Day 4

I spent time today being fully present and engaged with _____.
This is how I spent my time with him/her, and how
this time together made me feel...

_____

_____

_____

_____

_____

_____

_____

_____

_____

_____

_____

Day 5

I spent time today being fully present and engaged with _____.
This is how I spent my time with him/her, and how
this time together made me feel...

_____

_____

_____

_____

_____

_____

_____

_____

_____

_____

_____

_____

Day 6

I spent time today being fully present and engaged with _____.
This is how I spent my time with him/her, and how
this time together made me feel...

_____

_____

_____

_____

_____

_____

_____

_____

_____

_____

_____

Day 7

I spent time today being fully present and engaged with _____.
This is how I spent my time with him/her, and how
this time together made me feel...

_____

_____

_____

_____

_____

_____

_____

_____

_____

_____

_____

_____

_____

_____

Savoring Successes

*"Celebrate the journey. It's not all about the destination.
Savor all of your successes, even the small ones."*

Dawn Gluskin

Our successes in life bring us a wellspring of joy, pride, motivation, and satisfaction, but often these feelings are fleeting, even for our most brilliant achievements. We tend to gobble down life's most savory moments instead of sitting back and drinking them in. Our minds scurry to the next opportunity, the next win, the next big goal, leaving our recent triumph languishing in the dust.

Sometimes we diminish smaller successes because they feel like forgettable stepping-stones to our "real" achievements. The simple moments when we show kindness, complete a task, or follow through on a promise are tiny jewels of goodness that should be celebrated.

This week, you will focus on your successes, both large and small, by reflecting on them in detail. As you think about these achievements, mentally put yourself back into the moment, relive each step, and savor the satisfying feeling of success.

Best time to journal: *morning or evening*

Day 1

The success I focus on today is_____.
This is what I remember and how it made me feel...

_____

_____

_____

_____

_____

_____

_____

_____

_____

_____

_____

_____

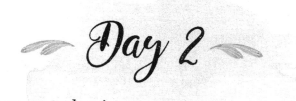

Day 2

The success I focus on today is_____.
This is what I remember and how it made me feel...

_____

_____

_____

_____

_____

_____

_____

_____

_____

_____

_____

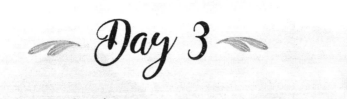

Day 3

The success I focus on today is_____.
This is what I remember and how it made me feel...

_____

_____

_____

_____

_____

_____

_____

_____

_____

_____

_____

_____

_____

Day 4

The success I focus on today is_____.
This is what I remember and how it made me feel...

_____

_____

_____

_____

_____

_____

_____

_____

_____

_____

_____

Day 5

The success I focus on today is_____.
This is what I remember and how it made me feel...

_____

_____

_____

_____

_____

_____

_____

_____

_____

_____

_____

_____

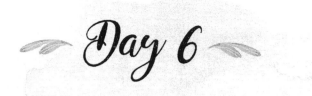

Day 6

The success I focus on today is_____.
This is what I remember and how it made me feel...

_____

_____

_____

_____

_____

_____

_____

_____

_____

_____

_____

_____

Day 7

The success I focus on today is_____.
This is what I remember and how it made me feel...

_____

_____

_____

_____

_____

_____

_____

_____

_____

_____

_____

_____

_____

WEEK 14

Connecting with Nature

> *"Nature's peace will flow into you as sunshine flows into trees. The winds will blow their own freshness into you, and the storms their energy, while cares will drop off like autumn leaves."*

John Muir

The beauty and simplicity of nature is what makes it so ideally suited to practicing mindfulness. Unlike our daily lives and the hectic world around us, nature's allure is often subtle. The light filtering through trees. The call of a bird. The wind rustling through leaves. These things quiet us and call us more deeply into ourselves.

The simple experience of walking outside in your own back yard is a great opportunity to practice mindfulness. Sights, smells, and sounds are ever present, yet often go unnoticed. When you pay attention, you discover a universe of bliss available to you in the intricacies and grandeur of the natural world.

This week you will strive to connect, appreciate and develop a relationship with the natural world around you using the journal prompts as your guide.

Best time to journal: *various times of day*

Day 1

*I walk outside and look at a tree. I stand a distance away from the tree
and focus all of my attention and senses on this tree. Then
I stand under the tree and focus from this perspective.
This is what I experienced with the tree...*

_____

_____

_____

_____

_____

_____

_____

_____

_____

_____

Day 2

Today I sit outside in a quiet spot in nature. I close my eyes and take a few deep, cleansing breaths. Then I just listen. I notice all of the sounds around me. This is what I heard and experienced by listening to nature...

_____

_____

_____

_____

_____

_____

_____

_____

_____

_____

Day 3

I take a blanket or towel outside and lie on my back. I look up at the clouds and observe them floating by. I noticed the shapes of clouds and what they remind me of. This is what I experienced noticing clouds today...

_____

_____

_____

_____

_____

_____

_____

_____

_____

_____

_____

Day 4

Today I grab a tote or bag and take a walk in the woods or a park. I look for natural objects that speak to me (a rock, a leaf, a piece of bark) and put them in my bag. This is what I collected, and what each item means to me...

_____

_____

_____

_____

_____

_____

_____

_____

_____

_____

_____

_____

Day 5

This evening I walk outside just before the sun is setting. I watch the light grow darker and see the changing colors of the sky. I notice how shadows and darkness change the landscape. This is what I noticed while watching the sunset...

Day 6

I go back to the woods or a park and focus my attention on living creatures. I attentively watch birds flying, squirrels scampering, and small insects in the grass. These are the creatures I noticed, and what they were doing...

_____

_____

_____

_____

_____

_____

_____

_____

_____

_____

_____

Day 7

Today I choose my own mindfulness activity in nature. This is what I did outside, and what I experienced...

_____

_____

_____

_____

_____

_____

_____

_____

_____

_____

_____

Practicing Self-Acceptance

"To be beautiful means to be yourself. You don't need to be accepted by others. You need to accept yourself."

Thích Nhất Hạnh

Underlying most of the emotional challenges we face—from depression to relationship problems—is the struggle for self-acceptance. When we don't feel worthy, we suffer, and with suffering we lose our ability to be present with ourselves and others.

Self-worth is essential for being a fully actualized individual. When we don't love ourselves, we compromise every part of our lives. We can't function at an optimal level and fulfill our potential for happiness and success.

A lack of self-acceptance can show up as anxiety, neediness, defensiveness, hypersensitivity, self-sabotaging behaviors, hyper-vigilance, perfectionism, a lack of boundaries, inauthenticity, and poor social skills. Through awareness of your feelings of low self-worth and how they manifest, you can make more conscious choices about how you perceive and treat yourself.

Best time to journal: *morning or evening*

Day 1

In what ways am I lacking self-acceptance?
How do I not like or love myself?

_____

_____

_____

_____

_____

_____

_____

_____

_____

_____

_____

Day 2

These are the things that the negative voice in my head tells me about the areas where I lack self-acceptance...

_____

_____

_____

_____

_____

_____

_____

_____

_____

_____

_____

Day 3

This is how my life would be different if I no longer judged myself harshly, and started accepting myself as I am...

_____

_____

_____

_____

_____

_____

_____

_____

_____

_____

_____

_____

Day 4

Today I am writing as my own best friend and biggest cheerleader.
This is what I want to say to me about my worthiness...

_____

_____

_____

_____

_____

_____

_____

_____

_____

_____

_____

Day 5

How do I define worthiness in myself and others?
What makes a person worthy of acceptance?

_____

_____

_____

_____

_____

_____

_____

_____

_____

_____

_____

_____

Day 6

Today I focus on a negative story I tell about myself (I'm unlovable, I have no friends, etc.). Then I challenge the story with evidence to the contrary. Here is my story and my contradictory evidence...

_____

_____

_____

_____

_____

_____

_____

_____

_____

_____

_____

Day 7

I choose to focus on my essential nature and the goodness inherent within me. These are the things I love about myself that make me unique and worthy...

_____

_____

_____

_____

_____

_____

_____

_____

_____

_____

_____

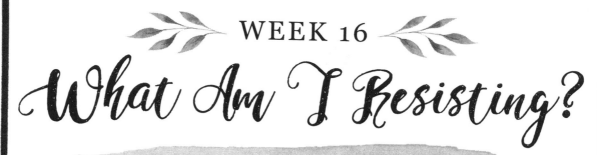

What Am I Resisting?

"Quit resisting. Let your pain pierce your hard heart so the agony can flow out and the love can rush in. It's the love that will bring you back to life."

Bryant McGill

Pain, uncertainty, and anxiety are uncomfortable emotions. We don't like to experience them, and often fear facing the deeper causes that trigger these feelings. In the moment, it seems more tolerable to push against discomfort, or to keep our heads buried in the sand so we don't have to face truth, vulnerability, or change.

When we resist whatever life presents to us, we lose our opportunity to be present with it. But when we are present with what frightens us, we are able to lessen the grip of resistance. We can shine a light of curiosity that allows us to move forward with clarity and confidence.

Awareness of what and where you are resisting gives you clues to where you need to grow. This week you will focus on what you are resisting, and examine why you are leaning away from life rather than leaning into it.

Best time to journal: *morning or evening*

Day 1

What positive changes or new habits in my life am I resisting,
and why am I resisting them?

_____

_____

_____

_____

_____

_____

_____

_____

_____

_____

_____

Day 2

In my relationship with _____, here is what I am resisting or avoiding, and what my higher self is calling on me to do about it...

_____

_____

_____

_____

_____

_____

_____

_____

_____

_____

_____

Day 3

*Here is what I fear facing from my past, and
how I resist dealing with it...*

_____

_____

_____

_____

_____

_____

_____

_____

_____

_____

_____

_____

Day 4

These are the aspects of my personality and behavior that I know I need to change, but I resist addressing them...

_____

_____

_____

_____

_____

_____

_____

_____

_____

_____

_____

Day 5

These are the beliefs and strong opinions that I am resistant to challenge or examine, and why I feel resistant...

_____

_____

_____

_____

_____

_____

_____

_____

_____

_____

_____

_____

Day 6

There are people in my life who hurt, offend, or manipulate me, but I resist addressing their behavior. These are the people, and this is why I am resistant to dealing with their behavior...

_____

_____

_____

_____

_____

_____

_____

_____

_____

_____

Day 7

How does my awareness of my own internal resistance impact my desire to push past resistance and take action? What would change in my life if I wasn't resistant to change, emotions, and vulnerability?

_____

_____

_____

_____

_____

_____

_____

_____

_____

_____

_____

_____

Positive Affirmations

"An affirmation opens the door. It's a beginning point on the path to change."

Louise Hay

Everything that we repeatedly say to ourselves aloud or in our thoughts are affirmations, whether they are disparaging or encouraging words. As a mindfulness habit, affirmations are positive phrases that you repeat to yourself describing who and how you want to be, using the present tense, as though the outcome has already occurred.

As you repeat the phrase, you are present with the reality of it, just as though it were already true. Used this way, affirmations can change the way we view the world, and even influence our actions.

When creating affirmations, use the present tense to focus on what you want, not on what you don't want. Rather than saying, "I don't want to be lonely anymore," you might say, "I have many loving and fulfilling relationships." Speak your affirmations out loud, meditate on them, and write about them in your journal. You can follow the affirmation prompts for each day, or create your own affirmations.

Best time to journal: *morning*

Day 1

My affirmation for today is: **I know what I want, and I'm not afraid to go after it**. *This is what I want and how I intend to go after it...*

_____

_____

_____

_____

_____

_____

_____

_____

_____

_____

_____

Day 2

My affirmation for today is: **I feel joy and contentment in this moment right now**. These are the ways I feel joy and contentment right now...

_____

_____

_____

_____

_____

_____

_____

_____

_____

_____

_____

Day 3

My affirmation for today is: **I easily find solutions to challenges and roadblocks, and move past them quickly**.

These are the challenges . . .

_____

_____

_____

_____

_____

_____

_____

_____

_____

_____

_____

_____

_____

Day 4

My affirmation for today is: **I trust myself and know my inner wisdom is my best guide**. *These are the ways I trust myself, and how my inner wisdom has guided me...*

_____

_____

_____

_____

_____

_____

_____

_____

_____

_____

_____

_____

Day 5

My affirmation for today is: **My world is a peaceful, loving, and joy-filled place to live**. These are the ways my world is peaceful, loving, and joy-filled...

_____

_____

_____

_____

_____

_____

_____

_____

_____

_____

_____

_____

_____

Day 6

My affirmation for today is: **My home is a peaceful sanctuary where I feel safe and happy**. This is how my home is peaceful, safe, and happy...

_____

_____

_____

_____

_____

_____

_____

_____

_____

_____

Day 7

My affirmation for today is: **I sow the seeds of peace wherever I go.** *This is how I sow the seeds of peace…*

_____

_____

_____

_____

_____

_____

_____

_____

_____

_____

_____

_____

_____

WEEK 18
Mindful Decluttering

"The best way to find out what we really need is to get rid of what we don't."

Marie Kondō

We so easily become attached to material possessions, allowing our homes and other spaces to become cluttered with every new whim, as well as years' worth of accumulated stuff. We mindlessly live with clutter, allowing it to slowly suck our mental and emotional energy.

Clutter reinforces our sense of overwhelm, stress, and emptiness, as we become "stuck" with these objects that don't fulfill us in the way we hoped they might.

As we mention in our book, *10-Minute Declutter,*

> *Clutter is often a reflection of our inner selves. If we feel disorganized, out of sorts, depressed, stressed out, or insecure, it shows up in the way we manage our daily lives. Organizing your clutter is a path to healing emotional blocks and inner confusion. As you reclaim control over your stuff, you'll feel better about yourself and have more positive energy.*

That's why adopting the practice of simplifying your spaces is such a life-changing mindfulness practice. If you maintain this activity consistently you can create a calm, peaceful environment that reinforces your other mindfulness habits.

Best time to journal: *morning or evening*

Day 1

Today I choose to declutter my _____.
I will spend _____ *minutes decluttering. This is my experience with*
decluttering today...

_____

_____

_____

_____

_____

_____

_____

_____

_____

_____

_____

Day 2

Today I choose to declutter my _____.
I will spend _____ minutes decluttering. This is my experience with
decluttering today...

_____

_____

_____

_____

_____

_____

_____

_____

_____

_____

_____

_____

_____

Day 3

Today I choose to declutter my _____ .
I will spend _____ *minutes decluttering. This is my experience with*
decluttering today...

_____

_____

_____

_____

_____

_____

_____

_____

_____

_____

_____

_____

_____

Day 4

Today I choose to declutter my _____.
I will spend _____ minutes decluttering. This is my experience with
decluttering today...

_____

_____

_____

_____

_____

_____

_____

_____

_____

_____

_____

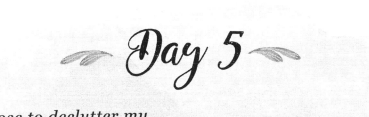

Day 5

Today I choose to declutter my _____.
I will spend _____ *minutes decluttering. This is my experience with decluttering today...*

_____

_____

_____

_____

_____

_____

_____

_____

_____

_____

_____

_____

_____

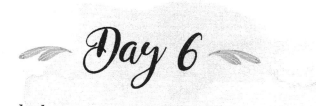

Day 6

Today I choose to declutter my _____.
I will spend _____ *minutes decluttering. This is my experience with decluttering today...*

_____

_____

_____

_____

_____

_____

_____

_____

_____

_____

_____

Day 7

Today I choose to declutter my _____.
I will spend _____ minutes decluttering. This is my experience with decluttering today...

_____

_____

_____

_____

_____

_____

_____

_____

_____

_____

_____

_____

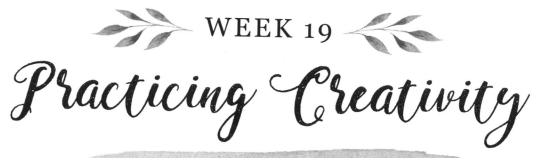

Practicing Creativity

"Don't think. Thinking is the enemy of creativity. It's self-conscious, and anything self-conscious is lousy. You can't try to do things. You simply must do things."

Ray Bradbury

We spoke at the beginning of this journal about the importance of non-judgment as a key element of mindfulness. An obvious barrier to creativity is that most of us tend edit our ideas and reject possibilities before exploring them fully. When we "try" to be creative, we are met by our own inner critic who throws cold water on our efforts, making us lose interest and focus.

Creative activities give us the chance to practice the kind of focused attention and presence that is inherent in mindfulness. Applying non-judgmental awareness to these endeavors frees you to fully explore your own creative landscape. This week, your focus will be on using creative activity as a gateway to mindfulness.

Prior to each activity outlined in the prompts, take a few moments to get into a meditative state. Close your eyes, then take a few deep and cleansing breaths until you feel calm and centered. Visualize yourself releasing all negativity and judgments as you prepare to enter a creative mindset. Allow yourself the freedom to explore each activity with joy and focus.

Best time to journal: *various times of day*

Day 1

I choose an everyday item from my home (a brush, the remote control, a light bulb, etc.) and ask myself, "What else can I do with this?" Here are my creative ideas for seeing other possibilities in this object.

_____

_____

_____

_____

_____

_____

_____

_____

_____

_____

_____

_____

_____

Day 2

Today I grab a blank sheet of paper and a pencil. I draw something (a tree, a face, an apple, anything I want) for 5 to 10 minutes without judging or erasing. This is my experience with focused drawing...

_____

_____

_____

_____

_____

_____

_____

_____

_____

_____

_____

_____

Day 3

Today I choose my favorite song and listen to it once. Then I replace the lyrics with my own. My song is _____.

Here are my new lyrics...

_____

_____

_____

_____

_____

_____

_____

_____

_____

_____

_____

_____

Day 4

I think about someone important to me who has made a difference in my life, and I write a poem about them. That person is _____.

Here is my poem...

_____

_____

_____

_____

_____

_____

_____

_____

_____

_____

Day 5

Today I write for 5 to 10 minutes in a stream of consciousness.
I write whatever comes to my head without judging or changing it.
Here is my writing...

_____

_____

_____

_____

_____

_____

_____

_____

_____

_____

_____

Day 6

Today I think about a problem, challenge, or goal that I have. I write down every possible idea I have for solving the problem, dealing with the challenge, or reaching the goal. Here is my problem, challenge, or goal, and my "brain dump" about it...

_____

_____

_____

_____

_____

_____

_____

_____

_____

_____

_____

Day 7

Using the phrase, "This is happiness," I draw a picture that reflects this statement using whatever comes to mind. This is what I drew, and how I chose this representation of the phrase...

_____

_____

_____

_____

_____

_____

_____

_____

_____

_____

_____

_____

_____

Practicing Forgiveness

"The truth is, unless you let go, unless you forgive yourself, unless you forgive the situation, unless you realize that the situation is over, you cannot move forward."

Steve Maraboli

Forgiving yourself or other people is not an easy undertaking. It's hard to let go of the mistakes we make and the regrets we nurture about ourselves. It's hard to release another person with the salve of forgiveness when our own wounds are still raw. But holding on to anger or regret for a prolonged time isn't beneficial for your well-being or ability to be present in the moment.

Anger locks you in the past, replaying slights you've endured from others or the mistakes you've made yourself. Only forgiveness can unlock you from sadness, rumination, and resentment, and lead to complete healing and wholeness. What if you could forgive what has happened in the past and focus on what is rather than what should have been?

Mindfulness around your suffering helps you accept others (and yourself) for who they are, with their own thoughts and reactions, without judging them as good or bad. It also shows you a way to let go of thoughts about what is "right" or "wrong" in how one thinks, feels, or experiences reality. Mindfulness gives you a choice about how you want to move forward, and puts control back into your hands.

Best time to journal: *morning or evening*

Day 1

I am having difficulty forgiving myself for _____.
These are the feelings I have about this situation, and
why I can't forgive myself...

_____

_____

_____

_____

_____

_____

_____

_____

_____

_____

_____

_____

Day 2

If I had the chance for a "re-do" with the situation I can't forgive myself for, this is how I would do things differently...

_____

_____

_____

_____

_____

_____

_____

_____

_____

_____

_____

Day 3

Today, I begin a meditation and think about this situation I can't forgive myself for. I allow any emotions to arise, and simply notice them. Then I offer myself full and complete forgiveness. This is what I experienced in this meditation...

_____

_____

_____

_____

_____

_____

_____

_____

_____

_____

_____

_____

Day 4

I am having difficulty forgiving _____
for_____. These are the feelings
I have about this situation, and why I can't forgive this person...

_____

_____

_____

_____

_____

_____

_____

_____

_____

_____

_____

_____

_____

_____

_____

_____

Day 5

Today I think about this person who hurt me, and I try to inhabit his/ her inner world. I strive to see the situation from his/her perspective. This is what I noticed...

_____

_____

_____

_____

_____

_____

_____

_____

_____

_____

_____

_____

Day 6

I think about the person who hurt me, and I ask myself, "What was my role in this situation? How did I contribute to my own suffering?" This is what I noticed...

_____

_____

_____

_____

_____

_____

_____

_____

_____

_____

_____

Day 7

Today I close my eyes and visualize my heart and mind softening toward this person. I see myself giving him/her a hug and offering my full and complete forgiveness. This is what I noticed...

_____

_____

_____

_____

_____

_____

_____

_____

_____

_____

_____

Finding Purpose

"Your purpose in life is to find your purpose and give your whole heart and soul to it."

Gautama Buddha

Sometimes it feels we are merely passengers on the bus to nowhere. We hop on early in our adult lives, and then mindlessly allow the bus to determine our direction in life. At times, the destination is fine, but too often it's not. It's boring and uninspired, with the same landscapes passing us every day. There is no purpose in life.

This happens because we are unconscious, not realizing we have the power to jump into the driver's seat and change directions. Once you're in the driver's seat, you must feel confident you know where you want to go, and why. The "why" of our lives is the force that inspires us, the internal motivator that creates energy and enthusiasm. Mindfulness about the "whys" in all areas of our lives gives us choice and direction based on our values and deepest desires.

Best time to journal: *morning or evening*

Day 1

Today I think about the values that I hold dear for my life, the values that I want my life to reflect. These are my values...

_____

_____

_____

_____

_____

_____

_____

_____

_____

_____

_____

Day 2

What is the "why" of my career? Why do I do the work I do?
If I have no "why," what would I like it to be?

_____

_____

_____

_____

_____

_____

_____

_____

_____

_____

_____

Day 3

What is the mark I want to make on the world and my community through my work?

_____

_____

_____

_____

_____

_____

_____

_____

_____

_____

_____

_____

_____

Day 4

What feels deeply important and meaningful to me?
How am I integrating these things into my life?

_____

_____

_____

_____

_____

_____

_____

_____

_____

_____

_____

_____

Day 5

*In my love relationship, what is the highest vision I have for
the way we connect and interact with one another?
What is the larger purpose of our relationship?*

_____

_____

_____

_____

_____

_____

_____

_____

_____

_____

_____

_____

Day 6

In my other important relationships, what is the highest vision
I have for the way we connect and interact with one another?
Who do I want to be in these relationships?

_____

_____

_____

_____

_____

_____

_____

_____

_____

_____

_____

_____

Day 7

What are some actions I need to take to align my life, work, and relationships with my values and my highest intentions for each area of my life? What changes do I need to make?

_____

_____

_____

_____

_____

_____

_____

_____

_____

_____

_____

_____

WEEK 22

Mindful Movement

"Movement is a medicine for creating change in a person's physical, emotional, and mental states."

Carol Welch

You already know the benefits of exercise—they are numerous and compelling. Despite knowing how beneficial movement is, most people don't have a regular fitness routine. We often see exercise as an uncomfortable chore, and we find a variety of excuses to avoid it.

Perhaps we see exercise as simply a difficult means to a healthier end, rather than an enjoyable endeavor in and of itself. Exercise can be an excellent mindfulness activity if you shift your thoughts about how you approach it. If you view it as a way to be present with your body and become more aware of your own physical abilities, you can lessen your resistance and enjoy being more intentional with your body and movements.

This week, you will focus on short (10- 20-minute) mindful movement activities to warm up your body and get your energy flowing. As you perform the exercises, imagine sending energy to the part or parts of your body performing the work. Don't judge your efforts. Just notice your body and how it feels.

Best time to journal: *morning or evening*

Day 1

Today I move my body by stretching. I stretch my neck, my arms, my fingers, my back, my legs, my ankles, my feet, and my toes. I breathe into each stretch, noticing how each part feels during and after the stretch. This is what I noticed about stretching...

_____

_____

_____

_____

_____

_____

_____

_____

_____

_____

_____

Day 2

*Today I stand on one foot with my arms outstretched for balance.
I notice how my body recalibrates to achieve balance. Then I bend at
the waist very slowly, reaching down to touch my toe while remaining
balanced. I do this exercise 10 times, alternating feet.
This is what I noticed as I focused on balance...*

_____

_____

_____

_____

_____

_____

_____

_____

_____

_____

Day 3

Today I turn on music, either fast or slow, suiting my mood. I dance to the music, allowing my body to flow with the energy of sound and rhythm. I focus intently on my body and the music as one.
This is what I noticed...

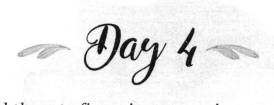

Day 4

Today I spend three to five minutes on vigorous aerobic activity (running in place, jumping jacks, jumping rope, etc.). I notice my increasing feelings of exhaustion and breathlessness, as well as feelings of burn or soreness in my muscles. I am completely in tune with my body throughout the activity. This is what I noticed...

_____

_____

_____

_____

_____

_____

_____

_____

_____

_____

_____

Day 5

Today I perform 15 walking lunges in one direction, and 15 in the other. I descend until my rear knee nearly touches the ground, while remaining upright, with my front knee above my front foot. I pay focused attention to each movement and the feelings in my body. This is what I noticed...

_____

_____

_____

_____

_____

_____

_____

_____

_____

_____

_____

_____

Day 6

Today I take a short walk outside. With each step, I pay attention to the lifting and falling of my foot and the movement in my legs and body. I notice any shifting of my body from side to side. I notice my breathing. Whatever else captures my attention, I come back to the sensation of walking. This was my experience with mindful walking...

_____

_____

_____

_____

_____

_____

_____

_____

_____

_____

_____

_____

Day 7

Today I choose a physical activity that I prefer. I focus my attention on my breathing, the sensations in my body, my balance, and my coordination. I notice and observe how my body responds during this activity. This is what I noticed...

_____

_____

_____

_____

_____

_____

_____

_____

_____

_____

_____

_____

My Favorite Things

"I want to live my life in such a way that it colors my things with memories."

Marie Kondo

In her book *Spark Joy*, author Marie Kondo invites us to be mindfully discerning about the material objects we keep around us, in our homes and other spaces.

As she says in her book, "Discarding is not the point; what matters is keeping those things that bring you joy. If you discard everything until you have nothing left but an empty house, I don't think you'll be happy living there. Our goal in tidying should be to create a living environment filled with the things we love."

Do the things in your home spark joy for you? Or do they seem like inanimate objects that have no meaning or purpose, and simply fill space? As you look around your home, car, or office, ask yourself if your possessions bring beauty into your life and stir your soul. Do they support a passion, interest, or hobby? Are they useful and necessary for day-to-day life? Are they meaningful or significant in some way?

This week you will choose things you own that spark joy in your life and write about why they bring you pleasure or satisfaction.

Best time to journal: *morning or evening*

Day 1

One of my favorite things is my_____.
This is why it sparks joy in my life, and why I like it so much...

_____

_____

_____

_____

_____

_____

_____

_____

_____

_____

_____

_____

Day 2

One of my favorite things is my_____.
This is why it sparks joy in my life, and why I like it so much...

_____

_____

_____

_____

_____

_____

_____

_____

_____

_____

_____

Day 3

One of my favorite things is my_____.
This is why it sparks joy in my life, and why I like it so much...

_____

_____

_____

_____

_____

_____

_____

_____

_____

_____

_____

_____

_____

_____

Day 4

One of my favorite things is my_____.
This is why it sparks joy in my life, and why I like it so much...

_____

_____

_____

_____

_____

_____

_____

_____

_____

_____

_____

Day 5

One of my favorite things is my_____.
This is why it sparks joy in my life, and why I like it so much...

_____

_____

_____

_____

_____

_____

_____

_____

_____

_____

_____

_____

Day 6

One of my favorite things is my_____.
This is why it sparks joy in my life, and why I like it so much...

_____

_____

_____

_____

_____

_____

_____

_____

_____

_____

_____

_____

Day 7

One of my favorite things is my_____.
This is why it sparks joy in my life, and why I like it so much...

_____

_____

_____

_____

_____

_____

_____

_____

_____

_____

_____

_____

_____

Empathic Listening

> *"Genuine listening is hard work; there is little about it that is mechanical... We hear with our ears, but we listen with our eyes and mind and heart and skin and guts as well."*

Alfred Benjamin

Empathic listening is mindful listening. It is listening with the intention of understanding, compassion, and presence without judgment. When you listen empathically, it's all about the other person and what they are trying to communicate—with their words, with the words left unspoken, and with their emotions.

Empathic listening requires a willingness to put yourself in the shoes of the other person so they feel heard in a non-judgmental way. It allows the speaker to feel safe, acknowledged, and valued. Your goal is to empower the speaker to greater self-awareness simply through your willingness to hear them.

As an empathic listener, you are in the moment with the speaker, completely attentive to what this person is saying, without interrupting or inserting your opinion. You ask open-ended questions that invite more from the speaker, and reflect back to him or her what you heard them say. This week you will look for opportunities to practice mindful listening with various people in your life.

Best time to journal: *various times of day*

Day 1

Today I listened empathically to _____.
Here is what he/she shared with me, and how I felt during
my time listening...

_____

_____

_____

_____

_____

_____

_____

_____

_____

_____

_____

Day 2

Today I listened empathically to _____.
Here is what he/she shared with me, and how I felt during my time listening...

_____

_____

_____

_____

_____

_____

_____

_____

_____

_____

_____

_____

Day 3

Today I listened empathically to _____.
Here is what he/she shared with me, and how I felt during
my time listening...

_____

_____

_____

_____

_____

_____

_____

_____

_____

_____

_____

_____

_____

Day 4

Today I listened empathically to _____.
Here is what he/she shared with me, and how I felt during
my time listening...

_____

_____

_____

_____

_____

_____

_____

_____

_____

_____

_____

Day 5

Today I listened empathically to _____.
Here is what he/she shared with me, and how I felt during
my time listening...

_____

_____

_____

_____

_____

_____

_____

_____

_____

_____

_____

_____

_____

Day 6

Today I listened empathically to _____.
Here is what he/she shared with me, and how I felt during
my time listening...

_____

_____

_____

_____

_____

_____

_____

_____

_____

_____

_____

_____

Day 7

Today I listened empathically to _____.
Here is what he/she shared with me, and how I felt during
my time listening...

_____

_____

_____

_____

_____

_____

_____

_____

_____

_____

_____

_____

_____

Notice Distractions

"When we clutter our lives with imagined obligations, unnecessary activities, and distractions that only kill time, we dilute the power of our lives."

Anne Katherine

Distraction is the undoing of mindfulness. You can't be focused in the moment when you are multitasking or being pulled away by various enticements.

In our technology-centered lives, we're constantly faced with distractions. They come from your digital devices, television, other people, and even your own intrusive thoughts. Each distraction harnesses control of your attention and resources, undermining your productivity and inner peace.

The solution is recognizing how mindfulness serves your goals by improving your focus and concentration. Become more aware of how distractions are infiltrating your daily activities, pulling you away from the task at hand. In the same way you refocus your attention on your breath during meditation, you can turn your attention away from distractions and back to the present moment.

Best time to journal: *various times of day*

Day 1

Today I wear a rubber band on my wrist to remind me to notice how often I'm distracted from my tasks, conversations, or work.
This is what I noticed about distractions, and how they impact me...

_____

_____

_____

_____

_____

_____

_____

_____

_____

_____

_____

_____

Day 2

Today I turn off my phone during a task or project that takes an hour or more. I put my phone away and don't look at it until I am done. This is what I noticed about being disconnected from my phone...

_____

_____

_____

_____

_____

_____

_____

_____

_____

_____

_____

 Day 3

Today I notice how other people in my life knowingly or unknowingly distract or interrupt me when I am trying to focus. This is what I noticed about other people, and these are the boundaries I want to create with them...

_____

_____

_____

_____

_____

_____

_____

_____

_____

_____

_____

_____

Day 4

Today I pay special attention to distractions on my computer. How often do I want to click away from my work to look at email, social media, or something else? This is what I noticed, and my plan to stay focused when I work on my computer...

_____

_____

_____

_____

_____

_____

_____

_____

_____

_____

_____

Day 5

Today I focus on how much I put on my plate daily, and any feelings of stress, agitation, or overwhelm due to my mounting obligations.
This is what I noticed...

_____

_____

_____

_____

_____

_____

_____

_____

_____

_____

_____

_____

_____

_____

Day 6

Today I choose to focus on two things—one in the morning and one in the afternoon. I will remove all distractions and let those around me know that I'm unavailable. This is what happened, and what I accomplished...

_____

_____

_____

_____

_____

_____

_____

_____

_____

_____

_____

_____

Day 7

Today I set aside time for rest and relaxation. I put aside work, tasks, digital devices, and television, and enjoy an experience in which I can immerse myself completely. This is what I did, and what I noticed...

_____

_____

_____

_____

_____

_____

_____

_____

_____

_____

_____

_____

Outcome-Directed Thinking

"If you don't make the time to work on creating the life you want, you're eventually going to be forced to spend a lot of time dealing with a life you don't want."

Kevin Ngo

Often, we try to solve a problem, approach a task, or set a goal with an unproductive mindset. We focus on the potential problems rather than the outcomes we want to achieve. We don't mindfully consider where our focus should be, the opportunities available to us, and the various possibilities for achieving what we want.

Using outcome-directed thinking, you can break free from this cycle to move forward creatively by focusing on what you want rather than the obstacles. Outcome-directed thinking is a more intentional, focused way of getting what you desire.

This week you will focus on outcome-directed thinking related to specific goals or challenges in your life. As you approach each one, ask yourself these five questions:

1. What do I want to achieve with this goal or problem?
2. How will I know when I've reached the goal or outcome?
3. What will I gain or lose by achieving this outcome? Is it worthwhile?
4. What resources do I need to achieve this outcome, and how will I get them?
5. What is the first step I can take to achieve this outcome?

Best time to journal: *morning*

Day 1

Today I focus on a goal, task, or problem, and the outcome I want to achieve using the five questions. This is the goal, task, or problem, and my answers to the questions...

_____

_____

_____

_____

_____

_____

_____

_____

_____

_____

_____

_____

Day 2

Today I focus on a goal, task, or problem, and the outcome I want to achieve using the five questions. This is the goal, task, or problem, and my answers to the questions...

_____

_____

_____

_____

_____

_____

_____

_____

_____

_____

_____

Day 3

Today I focus on a goal, task, or problem, and the outcome I want to achieve using the five questions. This is the goal, task, or problem, and my answers to the questions...

_____

_____

_____

_____

_____

_____

_____

_____

_____

_____

_____

_____

_____

Day 4

Today I focus on a goal, task, or problem, and the outcome I want to achieve using the five questions. This is the goal, task, or problem, and my answers to the questions...

_____

_____

_____

_____

_____

_____

_____

_____

_____

_____

Day 5

Today I focus on a goal, task, or problem, and the outcome I want to achieve using the five questions. This is the goal, task, or problem, and my answers to the questions...

_____

_____

_____

_____

_____

_____

_____

_____

_____

_____

_____

_____

Day 6

Today I focus on a goal, task, or problem, and the outcome I want to achieve using the five questions. This is the goal, task, or problem, and my answers to the questions...

_____

_____

_____

_____

_____

_____

_____

_____

_____

_____

_____

Day 7

Today I focus on a goal, task, or problem, and the outcome I want to achieve using the five questions. This is the goal, task, or problem, and my answers to the questions...

_____

_____

_____

_____

_____

_____

_____

_____

_____

_____

_____

_____

_____

_____

_____

Find Your Flow State

"It is how we choose what we do, and how we approach it, that will determine whether the sum of our days adds up to a formless blur, or to something resembling a work of art."

Mihaly Csikszentmihalyi

Is it possible to be in a meditative state when you are working? Can you be mindful while performing a task, hobby, or project? When you become so immersed in an activity that nothing else seems to matter, you fall into a "state of flow" in which you lose your sense of self and even lose track of time. Flow is the ultimate form of mindfulness in action.

During a flow state, you find great inner clarity as you are performing the activity. You are so engaged that all distractions fall away, and you are one with the task at hand—whether it's crafting your annual goals, writing your book, or preparing a new recipe.

This is the state of mind you want to achieve with any focused effort you perform at work or in your personal life. You can best achieve this state with activities that are somewhat challenging (but not extremely difficult), and that you enjoy doing. Be sure to eliminate distractions, and set aside at least 10 to 20 minutes to get into the flow state and lose yourself in your efforts.

Best time to journal: *afternoon or evening*

Day 1

*Today I focused on getting into the flow state. This is the activity
I worked on, and my experience with being in flow...*

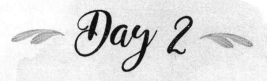

Day 2

Today I focused on getting into the flow state. This is the activity
I worked on, and my experience with being in flow...

_____

_____

_____

_____

_____

_____

_____

_____

_____

_____

_____

Day 3

Today I focused on getting into the flow state. This is the activity
I worked on, and my experience with being in flow...

_____

_____

_____

_____

_____

_____

_____

_____

_____

_____

_____

_____

Day 4

Today I focused on getting into the flow state. This is the activity I worked on, and my experience with being in flow...

_____

_____

_____

_____

_____

_____

_____

_____

_____

_____

_____

Day 5

*Today I focused on getting into the flow state. This is the activity
I worked on, and my experience with being in flow...*

_____

_____

_____

_____

_____

_____

_____

_____

_____

_____

_____

_____

Day 6

Today I focused on getting into the flow state. This is the activity
I worked on, and my experience with being in flow...

_____

_____

_____

_____

_____

_____

_____

_____

_____

_____

_____

_____

Day 7

Today I focused on getting into the flow state. This is the activity I worked on, and my experience with being in flow...

_____

_____

_____

_____

_____

_____

_____

_____

_____

_____

_____

_____

_____

Practice Slow Work

"For the overachievers out there: Your mantra is likely, 'What else can I do today?' Consider replacing that for a week with, 'What can I do less of today?' and see what happens."

Tad Hargrove

A vital element of being present in the moment is simply slowing down with everything you do. When you rush from one thing to the next, trying to cram in as much effort as possible, you lose the sense of joy and flow that comes with the process, the practice, and the action.

In a society that places high value on multitasking and productivity, slowing down might make you feel like you're not doing or accomplishing enough. But taking more time to thoroughly complete a task or sit with an experience will ultimately make you more productive, creative, and happy.

This week, rather than racing to check everything off your list, make a conscious decision to slow down in all of your endeavors—whether it's washing dishes or completing a project at work. Do one thing at a time, and give yourself more time to complete each activity. Rather than focusing on speed, shift your focus to thoroughness and excellence. Try to enjoy the process rather than rushing to the result.

Best time to journal: *evening or before bed*

Day 1

Today I slowed down and gave myself plenty of time
to do _____. This is what
I experienced by slowing down and being
more focused and thorough...

_____

_____

_____

_____

_____

_____

_____

_____

_____

_____

_____

_____

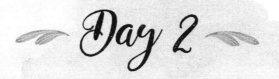

Day 2

*Today I slowed down and gave myself plenty of time
to do _____. This is what
I experienced by slowing down and being
more focused and thorough...*

_____

_____

_____

_____

_____

_____

_____

_____

_____

_____

_____

_____

Day 3

Today I slowed down and gave myself plenty of time
to do _____. This is what
I experienced by slowing down and being
more focused and thorough...

_____

_____

_____

_____

_____

_____

_____

_____

_____

_____

_____

_____

_____

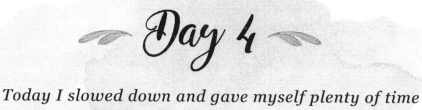

Day 4

Today I slowed down and gave myself plenty of time to do _____. This is what I experienced by slowing down and being more focused and thorough...

_____

_____

_____

_____

_____

_____

_____

_____

_____

_____

_____

_____

Day 5

Today I slowed down and gave myself plenty of time to do _____. This is what I experienced by slowing down and being more focused and thorough...

_____

_____

_____

_____

_____

_____

_____

_____

_____

_____

_____

_____

_____

_____

_____

Day 6

Today I slowed down and gave myself plenty of time to do _____. This is what I experienced by slowing down and being more focused and thorough...

_____

_____

_____

_____

_____

_____

_____

_____

_____

_____

_____

Day 7

Today I slowed down and gave myself plenty of time
to do _____. This is what
I experienced by slowing down and being
more focused and thorough...

_____

_____

_____

_____

_____

_____

_____

_____

_____

_____

_____

_____

Enhancing Self-Awareness

"By becoming self-aware, you gain ownership of reality; in becoming real, you become the master of both inner and outer life."

Deepak Chopra

When you seek self-awareness, you consciously and honestly tune in to your way of being in the world. You view yourself from the perspective of your higher, wiser self, observing your thoughts, choices, decisions, and actions. As you do this, you are compelled to decide whether the things you observe align with the person you want to be. Do your actions match with your integrity, your values, your purpose, your passions, your spirituality, and the core of who you are or who you want to be?

When you acknowledge where you are *not* fully authentic, you can act on the call from your higher consciousness to make better, wiser choices that lead to a more satisfying life. Enhance self-awareness and free yourself to experience the depths of joy, intimacy, authenticity, connection, peace, and fulfillment available to you.

This week, you will pay mindful attention to yourself and examine how you are not living in alignment with who you want to be. You will use your journaling time to consider the actions you need to take to recalibrate your life.

Best time to journal: *morning or evening*

Day 1

How do I struggle with a need to control certain people or aspects of my life? How is this holding me back? What do I need to change? What is one action I can take to improve?

_____

_____

_____

_____

_____

_____

_____

_____

_____

_____

_____

_____

Day 2

What unresolved issues do I have in my life? How are they impacting
me? What do I need to change? What is one action
I can take to improve?

_____

_____

_____

_____

_____

_____

_____

_____

_____

_____

_____

Day 3

How am I overly attached to substances, people, or behaviors?
How are these "addictions" holding me back? What do I need to change?
What is one action I can take to improve?

_____

_____

_____

_____

_____

_____

_____

_____

_____

_____

_____

_____

Day 4

What choices have I made that are pulling me down or not in my best interest? How are these choices holding me back? What do I need to change? What is one action I can take to improve?

_____

_____

_____

_____

_____

_____

_____

_____

_____

_____

_____

_____

Day 5

In what ways do I tend to react with anger, defensiveness, or self-pity?
How are these reactions holding me back? What do I need to change?
What is one action I can take to improve?

_____

_____

_____

_____

_____

_____

_____

_____

_____

_____

_____

_____

Day 6

In what areas of my life do I feel out of balance or agitated about the direction my life is going? How are these situations holding me back? What do I need to change? What is one action I can take to improve?

_____

_____

_____

_____

_____

_____

_____

_____

_____

_____

_____

_____

Day 7

What long-held beliefs or opinions do I hold that no longer reflect who I am? How do these beliefs or opinions hold me back? What do I need to change? What is one action I can take to improve?

_____

_____

_____

_____

_____

_____

_____

_____

_____

_____

_____

_____

Cultivate A Beginner's Mind

"In the beginner's mind there are many possibilities, but in the expert's there are few."

Shunryu Suzuki

What does it mean to cultivate a beginner's mind? It means you become willing to release entrenched mindsets about the way things should be or how you believe they are. You temporarily suspend all of your opinions, expectations, and strongly held beliefs so that you can explore an idea without mental limitations.

This openness allows you access to a deeper curiosity and heightened awareness of multiple possibilities for success in any endeavor or relationship. Your mind remains open to all options. Even if you are an expert in something, remaining open-minded lets you discover solutions or avenues you might not have previously realized existed. You can respond more mindfully and thoughtfully to circumstances in the moment, rather than just relying on past experience.

Best time to journal: *various timed of day*

Day 1

Today, as I approach a project or task, I ask myself, "How can I approach this project differently?" rather than immediately returning to standard operating procedures.
This is what I discovered...

_____

_____

_____

_____

_____

_____

_____

_____

_____

_____

_____

_____

_____

Day 2

Today I pay attention to how I pre-judge other people and make assumptions about them. This is how I challenge my assumptions about these people...

_____

_____

_____

_____

_____

_____

_____

_____

_____

_____

_____

_____

Day 3

Today I think about an area where I am an expert or highly skilled. I apply a beginner's mindset to this area and brainstorm new ways to approach my expertise. This is what I discovered...

_____

_____

_____

_____

_____

_____

_____

_____

_____

_____

_____

_____

Day 4

Today, I examine a failure from my past. Rather than seeing it negatively, I view it through a lens of curiosity, looking for information and lessons to expand me. This is what I discovered...

_____

_____

_____

_____

_____

_____

_____

_____

_____

_____

_____

_____

Day 5

Today I think about my strongly held beliefs related to politics, religion, or some other area of my life. I choose to look at the opposite perspective with curiosity and an open mind by reading or listening to another opinion. This is what I learned...

_____

_____

_____

_____

_____

_____

_____

_____

_____

_____

_____

_____

Day 6

Today I drop all labels and false identities about myself (like "I'm a mother," "I'm a consultant," "I'm a Democrat," etc.), and I look at myself with fresh eyes. This is who I am without labels...

_____

_____

_____

_____

_____

_____

_____

_____

_____

_____

_____

_____

Day 7

Today I walk outside and look at the world around me as though
I had been blind and now see for the first time. This is what
I observed and how I felt...

_____

_____

_____

_____

_____

_____

_____

_____

_____

_____

_____

_____

Mindful Boundaries

"Compassionate people ask for what they need. They say no when they need to, and when they say yes, they mean it. They're compassionate because their boundaries keep them out of resentment."

Brené Brown

Personal boundaries are the imaginary lines we draw around ourselves to maintain balance and protect our bodies, minds, emotions, and time from the behavior or demands of others. They provide the framework to keep us from being used or manipulated by others, and they allow us to confidently express who we are and what we want in life. They are an important part of our self-care.

Without healthy boundaries, you cannot have healthy relationships or feel authentic. You give up a part of yourself to be available or accommodating. Or you become so entangled with another person and their needs that you lose your own identity. Being intentional about what you will and won't accept from others allows you to be fully present with them without resentment or anxiety.

Best time to journal: *morning or evening*

Day 1

In what ways do I acquiesce to another's wishes when I don't really want to? How do I say "yes" when I mean "no," or vice versa? What do I need to do to change this?

_____

_____

_____

_____

_____

_____

_____

_____

_____

_____

_____

Day 2

How am I acting against my values or integrity in order to please someone else? What do I need to do to change this?

_____

_____

_____

_____

_____

_____

_____

_____

_____

_____

_____

_____

_____

Day 3

In what ways do I give too much in order to be perceived as useful or needed? What do I need to do to change this?

_____

_____

_____

_____

_____

_____

_____

_____

_____

_____

_____

_____

_____

Day 4

How do I allow myself to become overly involved in someone else's problems or difficulties to my detriment? What do I need to do to change this?

_____

_____

_____

_____

_____

_____

_____

_____

_____

_____

_____

Day 5

How am I not defining and communicating my emotional needs in my closest relationships, particularly with my spouse or partner? What do I need to do to change this?

_____

_____

_____

_____

_____

_____

_____

_____

_____

_____

_____

_____

Day 6

How am I adopting another person's beliefs, opinions, or ideas so I feel more accepted? What do I need to do to change this?

_____

_____

_____

_____

_____

_____

_____

_____

_____

_____

_____

_____

Day 7

What other boundaries do I need to communicate with those around me so I can be truer to myself?

_____

_____

_____

_____

_____

_____

_____

_____

_____

_____

_____

_____

_____

Your Relationship Vision

"I have sought love because in the union of love I have seen, in a mystic miniature, the prefiguring vision of the heaven that saints and poets have imagined."

Bertand Russell

Do you and your partner have goals and dreams about your relationship and life together as a couple? Do you know how you want to improve your connection and make it stronger? Crafting a relationship vision compels you to be more intentional in your connection, as you define your goals and expectations and create purpose and direction in your relationship.

A vision allows you to establish ground rules, boundaries, priorities, and plans for reaching your goals daily. It helps you bypass the conflicts that arise from divergent expectations by addressing them before they come up during conflict.

This week, you will focus on being mindful about the direction of your relationship and how you want to be as a partner or spouse. You will create a vision for several areas of your relationship, using the present tense and positive terms (what you want, not what you don't want). Even if you aren't in a relationship right now, you can prepare for one by having a vision for it.

Best time to journal: *morning or evening*

Day 1

This is my relationship vision for the way my partner and I deal with conflict and conflict resolution...

_____

_____

_____

_____

_____

_____

_____

_____

_____

_____

_____

_____

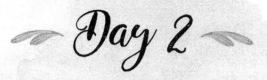

Day 2

This is my relationship vision for physical intimacy and affection with my partner...

_____

_____

_____

_____

_____

_____

_____

_____

_____

_____

_____

_____

Day 3

*This is my vision for the kind of emotional intimacy
my partner and I share...*

_____

_____

_____

_____

_____

_____

_____

_____

_____

_____

_____

_____

_____

_____

_____

Day 4

This is my vision for how we spend our time together for fun and relaxation...

_____

_____

_____

_____

_____

_____

_____

_____

_____

_____

_____

_____

Day 5

This is my vision for how we monitor and check in on the health of our relationship...

_____

_____

_____

_____

_____

_____

_____

_____

_____

_____

_____

_____

Day 6

This is my vision for how we deal with big decisions related to finances, purchases, parenting, etc....

_____

_____

_____

_____

_____

_____

_____

_____

_____

_____

_____

_____

Day 7

This is my vision for how we grow together and keep our relationship fresh, interesting, and deeply connected...

_____

_____

_____

_____

_____

_____

_____

_____

_____

_____

_____

_____

_____

Awareness of Attachments

"Attachment is the origin, the root of suffering; hence it is the cause of suffering."

Dalai Lama

Most days, we are stung by suffering over minor slights, failed opportunities, or disconnection from someone we love. We suffer over life's unpredictability. Sometimes, suffering expresses itself through irritability, anxiety, or agitation. Other times, it envelops us so completely we cannot separate ourselves from it.

In Buddhism, samsara, "the cycle of suffering," is a direct result of our desire for permanence and the need to control life through our attachments to things, people, and outcomes. No matter how hard we try, life remains unpredictable and suffering seems inevitable. But suffering also alerts us to the fact that we are not being aware of what we really are.

Whenever there is pain of any kind—grieving, loss, fear, resentment, jealousy, even physical pain—if you look deeply into that, you discover that behind the pain there is always something you're attached to. Through awareness of attachments and making efforts to let them go, you reduce suffering and gain a more peaceful acceptance of the present moment.

Best time to journal: *morning or evening*

Day 1

Today I contemplate the concept of attachment, and all of the things, people, and outcomes that I am attached to and cling to for fear of suffering without them. These are my attachments...

_____

_____

_____

_____

_____

_____

_____

_____

_____

_____

_____

Day 2

Today I contemplate my attachments right now, and the "why" behind them. Why am I attached to these things? What is the need or belief behind the attachment that binds me to them?

_____

_____

_____

_____

_____

_____

_____

_____

_____

_____

_____

_____

Day 3

Today I contemplate the effect my attachments have on me and my contentment in life. How do my attachments make me suffer?

Day 4

Today I contemplate the impermanence of all things, especially my attachments. How can the acceptance of impermanence make me more appreciative and present in my life?

_____

_____

_____

_____

_____

_____

_____

_____

_____

_____

_____

_____

Day 5

Today I consider my past attachments and whether or not they resulted in long-term peace and happiness. Did the things, people, and outcomes I desired in the past afford me on-going happiness?

_____

_____

_____

_____

_____

_____

_____

_____

_____

_____

_____

_____

Day 6

Today I pay attention to any mental suffering that shows up as stress, anxiety, frustration, anger, or any negative emotion.
What are the attachments behind my suffering?

_____

_____

_____

_____

_____

_____

_____

_____

_____

_____

_____

_____

Day 7

Today I contemplate life without attachments, and the ability to let go and savor "what is." This is how it would feel to live more in a state of non-attachment...

_____

_____

_____

_____

_____

_____

_____

_____

_____

_____

_____

_____

Kindness and Respect

"Remember there's no such thing as a small act of kindness. Every act creates a ripple with no logical end."

Scott Adams

In a world where aggression, animosity, and disregard seem to infiltrate our perceptions and awareness every day, it's easy to forget our universal connection to other human beings. We are careless with our words. We feel or act superior to those we deem beneath us. We neglect the most basic expressions of kindness and respect from those around us—from our family members to the people we pass on the street.

Showing kindness and respect to others—even those you don't like, or feel indifferent about—not only transforms the other person, but it also changes your perceptions of yourself and your ability to be fully present and connected to all people.

It is easy to be kind when life is going well. When we feel the world is against us, our habitual response is to strike back. Focusing on kindness and respect toward others trains our minds to let go of negative and habitual patterns, and allows us to cultivate an open-hearted, compassionate, and positive mindset.

Best time to journal: *evening or before bed*

Day 1

Today I focus on showing kindness and respect to my family members, even when they trigger frustration or anger. This is how I expressed kindness and respect to them, and what I experienced...

_____

_____

_____

_____

_____

_____

_____

_____

_____

_____

_____

_____

Day 2

Today I focus on showing kindness and respect to a service person I encounter during the day. This is how I expressed kindness and respect to them, and what I experienced...

_____

_____

_____

_____

_____

_____

_____

_____

_____

_____

_____

_____

Day 3

Today I practice a random act of kindness toward someone, expecting nothing in return. This is the act of kindness, and what I experienced...

_____

_____

_____

_____

_____

_____

_____

_____

_____

_____

_____

_____

Day 4

Today I focus on smiling and making eye contact with people I encounter throughout the day. This is what I experienced...

_____

_____

_____

_____

_____

_____

_____

_____

_____

_____

_____

_____

Day 5

Today I contemplate someone who has hurt or offended me, and think of all the ways he or she is deserving of respect and kindness.
These are the ways...

_____

_____

_____

_____

_____

_____

_____

_____

_____

_____

_____

_____

Day 6

Today I focus on sincerely complimenting people I encounter for something I notice or appreciate about them.
This is what I experienced...

_____

_____

_____

_____

_____

_____

_____

_____

_____

_____

_____

_____

Day 7

Today I think of my own way to show kindness and respect to one person, or several. This is how I expressed kindness and respect to them, and what I experienced...

_____

_____

_____

_____

_____

_____

_____

_____

_____

_____

_____

Noticing Moods

> *"Rain clouds and stormy moods take time to blow away, but sooner or later the sun always comes out."*

Shirley Parenteau

Every day you have moods and emotions that pass through you like clouds floating through the sky. Some moods stick with you for a few hours or even all day. Others are fleeting storms or rays of sunshine. Your daily moods are like internal weather—sometimes unpredictable, always changeable, rarely significant enough to give them too much attention.

But most of us get stuck in our moods—especially negative moods. We think, "I'm depressed. I'm angry. I'm lethargic. I'm not happy," and begin to associate our entire experience of the world through the lens of our moods. We create secondary suffering by resisting the emotions and the way our moods impact our day.

This week you will focus on simply noticing your moods throughout the day without judgment or self-blame. Pay attention to anything that might have triggered your mood, good or bad. Simply noticing the mercurial nature of your moods and being present with them will help you recognize how fleeting these feelings can be.

Best time to journal: *various times of day*

Day 1

These are the moods and emotions that I noticed today, what might have triggered them, and what I noticed about them...

Day 2

These are the moods and emotions that I noticed today, what might have triggered them, and what I noticed about them...

_____

_____

_____

_____

_____

_____

_____

_____

_____

_____

_____

_____

Day 3

These are the moods and emotions that I noticed today, what might have triggered them, and what I noticed about them...

_____

_____

_____

_____

_____

_____

_____

_____

_____

_____

_____

Day 4

These are the moods and emotions that I noticed today, what might have triggered them, and what I noticed about them...

_____

_____

_____

_____

_____

_____

_____

_____

_____

_____

_____

Day 5

These are the moods and emotions that I noticed today, what might have triggered them, and what I noticed about them...

_____

_____

_____

_____

_____

_____

_____

_____

_____

_____

_____

_____

Day 6

These are the moods and emotions that I noticed today, what might have triggered them, and what I noticed about them...

_____

_____

_____

_____

_____

_____

_____

_____

_____

_____

_____

_____

_____

_____

Day 7

These are the moods and emotions that I noticed today, what might have triggered them, and what I noticed about them...

_____

_____

_____

_____

_____

_____

_____

_____

_____

_____

_____

_____

_____

Practice Mindful Acceptance

"Life is a series of natural and spontaneous changes. Don't resist them; that only creates sorrow. Let reality be reality. Let things flow naturally forward in whatever way they like."

Lao Tzu

Things don't always go according to our expectations. People let us down. We encounter a challenging setback. An unexpected problem surprises us. Our first reaction when things go awry is to attempt to fix the situation. That's a useful response if change is possible, but many times a setback simply is what it is.

Often there's nothing to be done that can change the outcome or make things better right away. So our next reaction is to push against the reality of the situation. As we resist, we create more tension and suffering. We lose the opportunity for creative awareness about the situation.

By practicing acceptance of the negative situation and your reaction to it, you can find peace in moving forward. Mindful acceptance is not about giving up or disengaging. By accepting with a calm and focused mind, you may find that the problem is more complex or less difficult than you imagined. It may be dependent on other situations, or have roots in something deeper that you can't access when resisting.

Best time to journal: *morning or evening*

Day 1

Today I contemplate a current negative or challenging situation.
I notice how I am resisting this situation, and the emotions
I have around it. This is what I noticed...

_____

_____

_____

_____

_____

_____

_____

_____

_____

_____

_____

Day 2

I contemplate the same negative situation and the emotions I have about it. I practice calm acceptance of my emotions and the difficulty of the situation without resisting either. This is what I noticed...

_____

_____

_____

_____

_____

_____

_____

_____

_____

_____

_____

_____

_____

Day 3

As I practice acceptance of the situation, I ask myself,
"What could I be missing or not recognizing about this situation?"
This is what came up for me...

_____

_____

_____

_____

_____

_____

_____

_____

_____

_____

_____

_____

_____

Day 4

Today I ask myself if there's anything I can do to change or improve the situation. If so, here is a list of action steps I might take...

_____

_____

_____

_____

_____

_____

_____

_____

_____

_____

_____

_____

Day 5

If there are no actions I can take today to improve the situation, I visualize putting the problem into a helium balloon, releasing the balloon, and watching it float away and disappear out of sight. This is how I felt by releasing the problem...

_____

_____

_____

_____

_____

_____

_____

_____

_____

_____

_____

_____

Day 6

Today I check in with my emotions again about this situation,
and how they have evolved. Am I still resisting?
These are my thoughts and feelings about the situation...

_____

_____

_____

_____

_____

_____

_____

_____

_____

_____

_____

Day 7

Today I contemplate a past negative situation that I resisted and felt hopeless about. What was the outcome of the situation? How might mindful acceptance have helped me with this situation at the time?

_____

_____

_____

_____

_____

_____

_____

_____

_____

_____

_____

_____

Be An Objective Advisor

"There is a voice inside of you that whispers all day long, 'I feel this is right for me, I know that this is wrong.' No teacher, preacher, parent, friend or wise man can decide. What's right for you—just listen to the voice that speaks inside."

Shel Silverstein

We often encounter daily challenges that are complicated, confusing, and emotionally charged in relationships, at work, or just the activities of our day. That feeling of overwhelm can make it hard to have clarity to figure out the best next steps. Every choice feels fraught with potential negative consequences or unknown outcomes.

Getting outside feedback and advice can be helpful, but the best place to begin looking for solutions is within you. You can be your own coach or advisor by tapping into your inner wisdom and intuition, leading you to the best course of action.

A simple mindfulness technique can help you move forward to connect with your inner wisdom. Become "the observer" of your thoughts, as though a separate "you" is watching your thoughts in your mind. Drawing from this vantage point, change "the watcher" into the "objective advisor" who can draw from your observations and subconscious awareness to help you reach a sound conclusion or find a solution.

Best time to journal: *evening or before bed*

Day 1

I contemplate a challenge I encountered today or in the past. I visualize my wise objective advisor sitting next to me, and I ask, "How should I handle this situation?" This is what my advisor said...

_____

_____

_____

_____

_____

_____

_____

_____

_____

_____

_____

Day 2

I contemplate a challenge I encountered today or in the past. I visualize my wise objective advisor sitting next to me, and I ask, "How should I handle this situation?" This is what my advisor said...

_____

_____

_____

_____

_____

_____

_____

_____

_____

_____

Day 3

I contemplate a challenge I encountered today or in the past. I visualize my wise objective advisor sitting next to me, and I ask, "How should I handle this situation?" This is what my advisor said...

_____

_____

_____

_____

_____

_____

_____

_____

_____

_____

_____

_____

_____

_____

_____

Day 4

I contemplate a challenge I encountered today or in the past. I visualize my wise objective advisor sitting next to me, and I ask, "How should I handle this situation?" This is what my advisor said...

_____

_____

_____

_____

_____

_____

_____

_____

_____

_____

_____

Day 5

I contemplate a challenge I encountered today or in the past. I visualize my wise objective advisor sitting next to me, and I ask, "How should I handle this situation?" This is what my advisor said...

_____

_____

_____

_____

_____

_____

_____

_____

_____

_____

_____

Day 6

I contemplate a challenge I encountered today or in the past. I visualize my wise objective advisor sitting next to me, and I ask, "How should I handle this situation?" This is what my advisor said...

_____

_____

_____

_____

_____

_____

_____

_____

_____

_____

_____

_____

Day 7

I contemplate a challenge I encountered today or in the past. I visualize my wise objective advisor sitting next to me, and I ask, "How should I handle this situation?" This is what my advisor said...

_____

_____

_____

_____

_____

_____

_____

_____

_____

_____

_____

_____

_____

Re-Writing Your Story

"There is only one cause of unhappiness: the false beliefs you have in your head, beliefs so widespread, so commonly held, that it never occurs to you to question them."

Anthony de Mello

Throughout our lives, we create a number of stories about ourselves. Many of these stories are based on childhood and other past experiences, especially difficult experiences. As these experiences shaped our realities at the time, they also shaped our beliefs about the future.

We nurture these beliefs, even though they are no longer based in current reality. We create our own reality around them, stories we tell ourselves and others that keep us trapped in the past and limited in our growth. Only by challenging our stories and writing a new script for our lives can we escape the cycle of limiting beliefs, fears, and missed opportunities.

This week you will examine and challenge the stories you tell yourself and others about various parts of your life. You will look at how the story has limited you. Then you will write a new story to replace the old one.

Best time to journal: *morning or evening*

Day 1

Here is a story I tell myself, and the evidence that this story is no longer true for me. How has my story limited me in the past?
What is my new story?

_____

_____

_____

_____

_____

_____

_____

_____

_____

_____

_____

Day 2

Here is a story I tell myself, and the evidence that this story is no longer true for me. How has my story limited me in the past?
What is my new story?

_____

_____

_____

_____

_____

_____

_____

_____

_____

_____

_____

_____

Day 3

Here is a story I tell myself, and the evidence that this story is no longer true for me. How has my story limited me in the past?
What is my new story?

_____

_____

_____

_____

_____

_____

_____

_____

_____

_____

_____

_____

_____

_____

Day 4

Here is a story I tell myself, and the evidence that this story is no longer true for me. How has my story limited me in the past? What is my new story?

_____

_____

_____

_____

_____

_____

_____

_____

_____

_____

_____

_____

Day 5

Here is a story I tell myself, and the evidence that this story is no longer true for me. How has my story limited me in the past?
What is my new story?

_____

_____

_____

_____

_____

_____

_____

_____

_____

_____

_____

_____

Day 6

Here is a story I tell myself, and the evidence that this story is no longer true for me. How has my story limited me in the past? What is my new story?

_____

_____

_____

_____

_____

_____

_____

_____

_____

_____

_____

_____

Day 7

Here is a story I tell myself, and the evidence that this story is no longer true for me. How has my story limited me in the past?
What is my new story?

_____

_____

_____

_____

_____

_____

_____

_____

_____

_____

_____

_____

Listen to Music Mindfully

"Music gives a soul to the universe, wings to the mind, flight to the imagination, and life to everything."

Plato

Listening to music is a powerful mindfulness practice that can reduce stress, elevate your mood, raise your IQ, and offer many other mental benefits. Taking time to mindfully listen to music helps you return to your daily activities in a more positive, peaceful, and productive frame of mind.

Music is more than pleasant background noise. Actively listening to music without distraction is a portal to our inner worlds, allowing us to better understand our thoughts. It's a powerful art form that spans social, political, and language barriers, touching common experiences that are beyond words.

Music can also be healing, energizing, calming, and enlightening. It opens deep parts of us that we might not otherwise access when we allow ourselves to be fully immersed in the experience of immersive listening. This week you will mindfully listen to various types of music, and journal about your feelings and experiences.

Best time to journal: *any time of day*

Day 1

Today I choose a piece of classical music, remove all distractions, put on headphones, close my eyes, and listen with full focus and feeling.
This was my experience...

_____

_____

_____

_____

_____

_____

_____

_____

_____

_____

_____

Day 2

Today I choose a piece of jazz music, remove all distractions, put on headphones, close my eyes, and listen with full focus and feeling.
This was my experience...

_____

_____

_____

_____

_____

_____

_____

_____

_____

_____

_____

_____

_____

Day 3

Today I choose a piece of folk music, remove all distractions, put on headphones, close my eyes, and listen with full focus and feeling. This was my experience...

_____

_____

_____

_____

_____

_____

_____

_____

_____

_____

_____

_____

Day 4

Today I choose a piece of blues music, remove all distractions, put on headphones, close my eyes, and listen with full focus and feeling. This was my experience...

_____

_____

_____

_____

_____

_____

_____

_____

_____

_____

_____

_____

_____

Day 5

*Today I choose a piece of R&B or soul music, remove all distractions,
put on headphones, close my eyes, and listen with full focus and feeling.
This was my experience...*

_____

_____

_____

_____

_____

_____

_____

_____

_____

_____

Day 6

Today I choose a piece of rock music, remove all distractions, put on headphones, close my eyes, and listen with full focus and feeling. This was my experience...

_____

_____

_____

_____

_____

_____

_____

_____

_____

_____

_____

Day 7

*Today I choose a piece of my favorite music, remove all distractions,
put on headphones, close my eyes, and listen with full focus and feeling.
This was my experience...*

_____

_____

_____

_____

_____

_____

_____

_____

_____

_____

_____

_____

Cultivate Humility

> *"If you are humble, nothing will touch you, neither praise nor disgrace, because you know what you are."*
>
> Mother Teresa

Humility is often an underrated quality. Certainly in Western culture, and particularly in today's political climate, humility might be viewed as a sign of weakness.

However, many spiritual traditions, like Buddhism, view the cultivation of humility as a necessary step on the path toward enlightenment. If fact, humility, gratitude, and mindfulness are intrinsically intertwined. The word "humility" comes from the Latin word humilis, which means "grounded."

When you are humble, you don't need to show off, act defensive, or toot your own horn. You have a sense of confident neutrality about who you are as compared to others. You view your own strengths and weaknesses accurately, and recognize that everyone has intrinsic value—even those who appear "beneath" you in some way.

Best time to journal: *any time of day*

Day 1

Today I contemplate my strengths and weaknesses, and view them the way a loving friend would describe me—with honesty and clarity, unfiltered by ego or defensiveness.
These are my strengths and weakness...

_____

_____

_____

_____

_____

_____

_____

_____

_____

_____

_____

_____

_____

Day 2

Today I remember people who have helped me develop my strengths, and those who have supported me in areas where I'm weaker. I focus on gratitude for these people. These are the people and how they have supported me...

_____

_____

_____

_____

_____

_____

_____

_____

_____

_____

_____

_____

Day 3

Today I reflect on how I have fallen short of my own expectations or the expectations of others. How have these experiences humbled me and made me more grounded?

_____

_____

_____

_____

_____

_____

_____

_____

_____

_____

Day 4

Today I consider people around me who might be younger, less experienced, less driven, less successful, or less knowledgeable than me. What can I learn from them?

_____

_____

_____

_____

_____

_____

_____

_____

_____

_____

_____

_____

Day 5

Today I notice any feelings of judgment, defensiveness, insecurity, or pride I am holding on to. How can humility help me resolve or dissolve these feelings?

Day 6

Today I focus on praising others for their skills and accomplishments.
Wherever I go, I look for ways to offer praise.
This is what I noticed...

_____

_____

_____

_____

_____

_____

_____

_____

_____

_____

_____

_____

Day 7

Today I focus on serving others (my family, a friend, a co-worker) without expectation of a reward or return favor. This is how I served, and what I experienced...

_____

_____

_____

_____

_____

_____

_____

_____

_____

_____

_____

_____

_____

Practice a Growth Mindset

"You're in charge of your mind. You can help it grow by using it in the right way."

Carol Dweck

Dr. Carol Dweck, a leading expert in the field of motivation, has spent decades researching achievement and success, and through her research she's discovered something groundbreaking—the power of your mindset. A major factor in our happiness and success is whether we have a "fixed" mindset or a "growth" mindset.

Those with a fixed mindset believe their intelligence and abilities are set in stone, so they view failure as a direct measure of their competence and self-worth. They need to appear smart and capable, and want to avoid failure at all costs.

Those with a growth mindset believe change is possible, and even necessary. Failures are viewed as opportunities for learning. With a growth mindset, you are comfortable taking risks and challenging yourself. A growth mindset creates a love of learning and a resilience that's essential for great accomplishment.

Reinforcing a growth mindset in all your endeavors also supports mindfulness. With a growth mindset, you aren't impeded by concerns about the past or future. You give attention to the present moment by being spacious, flexible and open to new possibilities, and stretching beyond your limiting beliefs with focused attention in the now.

Best time to journal: *various times of day*

Day 1

Today I ask myself how I have reinforced a fixed mindset. How have I reacted to challenges, failures, or opportunities for taking risk in the past?

_____

_____

_____

_____

_____

_____

_____

_____

_____

_____

_____

_____

Day 2

What limiting beliefs or events trigger a fixed mindset within me?
What challenges or risks make me feel insecure?

_____

_____

_____

_____

_____

_____

_____

_____

_____

_____

_____

Day 3

In what ways am I now avoiding challenges or opportunities because I fear failure?

_____

_____

_____

_____

_____

_____

_____

_____

_____

_____

_____

_____

Day 4

Today I look for opportunities to practice a growth mindset by challenging myself to try something difficult, or stretching myself beyond my perceived limits. This is what happened...

_____

_____

_____

_____

_____

_____

_____

_____

_____

_____

_____

_____

_____

Day 5

Today I practice being a curious learner by asking more questions and being more curious about everyone I meet. This is what I discovered...

_____

_____

_____

_____

_____

_____

_____

_____

_____

_____

_____

Day 6

Today I focus on enjoying and valuing the process of a project or task rather than focusing on the end result. This is what I noticed...

_____

_____

_____

_____

_____

_____

_____

_____

_____

_____

_____

_____

Day 7

Today I reflect on taking ownership of my attitude to reinforce a growth mindset. This is how I will change my perspective on challenges, failure, limiting beliefs, and learning going forward...

_____

_____

_____

_____

_____

_____

_____

_____

_____

_____

_____

_____

Practice Mindful Speaking

> *"You are master of what you say until you utter it. Once you deliver it, you are its captive. Preserve your tongue as you do your gold and money. One word could bring disgrace and the termination of a bliss."*

Hazrat Ali ibn Abu-Talib

Being aware of the words you speak and how you say them is as important as being aware of your thoughts. In fact, there are facets of your mind that don't reveal themselves until you speak them out loud. When you are mindful of what motivates your speaking, you'll discover parts of your inner world that you might not access while by yourself or in meditation.

The Buddha provided five criteria that must be met when you speak—to speak what is true, kind, necessary, timely, and conducive to good will.

Using these mindful criteria, you will be less likely to say something you later regret and more likely to speak with wisdom and consideration. Remaining mindful while speaking gives you more choice in what you say, and leads you to a more compassionate, present way of interacting.

Speaking can be a challenging area in which to be mindful because of the emotions that come into play with other people. By being more attentive while speaking, you can grow in self-awareness. This week, consider why you say what you do, and what motivations prompt you to speak. Think about the emotions and feelings that influence your words, and reflect on the goals you want to achieve with your speaking. You might wear a rubber band on your wrist to remind you to pay attention to your words.

Best time to journal: *evening or before bed*

Day 1

Today I am conscious of pausing before I speak and ask myself, "Are my words true, kind, necessary, timely, and conducive to good will?" This is what I noticed with mindful speaking...

_____

_____

_____

_____

_____

_____

_____

_____

_____

_____

_____

_____

Day 2

Today I am conscious of pausing before I speak and ask myself, "Are my words true, kind, necessary, timely, and conducive to good will?" This is what I noticed with mindful speaking...

_____

_____

_____

_____

_____

_____

_____

_____

_____

_____

_____

_____

Day 3

Today I am conscious of pausing before I speak and ask myself, "Are my words true, kind, necessary, timely, and conducive to good will?" This is what I noticed with mindful speaking...

_____

_____

_____

_____

_____

_____

_____

_____

_____

_____

_____

_____

Day 4

Today I am conscious of pausing before I speak and ask myself, "Are my words true, kind, necessary, timely, and conducive to good will?" This is what I noticed with mindful speaking...

_____

_____

_____

_____

_____

_____

_____

_____

_____

_____

_____

Day 5

Today I am conscious of pausing before I speak and ask myself, "Are my words true, kind, necessary, timely, and conducive to good will?" This is what I noticed with mindful speaking...

_____

_____

_____

_____

_____

_____

_____

_____

_____

_____

_____

_____

Day 6

Today I am conscious of pausing before I speak and ask myself, "Are my words true, kind, necessary, timely, and conducive to good will?" This is what I noticed with mindful speaking...

_____

_____

_____

_____

_____

_____

_____

_____

_____

_____

_____

_____

Day 7

Today I am conscious of pausing before I speak and ask myself, "Are my words true, kind, necessary, timely, and conducive to good will?" This is what I noticed with mindful speaking...

_____

_____

_____

_____

_____

_____

_____

_____

_____

_____

_____

_____

Sowing Seeds of Peace

"We need to take action to develop compassion, to create inner peace within ourselves, and to share that inner peace with our family and friends. Peace and warm-heartedness can then spread through the community just as ripples radiate out across the water when you drop a pebble into a pond."

Dalai Lama

Every day we are faced with headlines of unimaginable violence, cruelty, and discord in our world and our own backyards. We hear stories of children bullying each other. We watch our adult leaders behaving like bullies and inciting conflict. Global peace, and even peace in our own communities, feels like an unattainable fantasy.

How is it possible to attain the inner peace that mindfulness promises when there is so much brutality and hatred all around us? How can we promote peace in such a badly broken world? The situation is not as hopeless as it might appear. We do have the power to promote peace in our own small circles, knowing that the ripples of peace can spread far and wide.

Mindfulness teaches us that peaceful minds lead to peaceful speech and actions. Many religions believe that the minds of all living beings are interconnected, so that our most insignificant thoughts have some effect on all other beings.

Consider this: What if each thought you have brings the world either a little closer to more violence or a little closer to peace? This week you will focus on using a peaceful mind and peaceful actions to nurture peace in the world.

Best time to journal: *various times of day*

Day 1

Today I focus on cultivating inner peace and equanimity by noticing negative thoughts and emotions that cause internal storms, and instead focus on gratitude and acceptance.
This is what I noticed through my efforts...

_____

_____

_____

_____

_____

_____

_____

_____

_____

_____

_____

_____

Day 2

Today I cultivate peace in the world by sowing seeds of peace with my family, friends, and co-workers. I am mindful of my actions, words, and thoughts around them. This is what I noticed through my efforts...

_____

_____

_____

_____

_____

_____

_____

_____

_____

_____

_____

_____

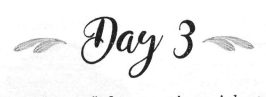

Day 3

Today I decide to "tune out" the negative, violent information that comes my way through my digital devices or television. This is how I detached from negativity today, and what I noticed through my efforts...

_____

_____

_____

_____

_____

_____

_____

_____

_____

_____

_____

_____

Day 4

Today I contemplate my own prejudices and entrenched beliefs about other races, cultures, religions, and customs. I make a point to read and educate myself more about my prejudices. This is what I noticed through my efforts...

_____

_____

_____

_____

_____

_____

_____

_____

_____

_____

_____

_____

Day 5

Today I spread peace by showing a child or another person how to achieve calm through deep and mindful breathing.
This is what I noticed through my efforts...

_____

_____

_____

_____

_____

_____

_____

_____

_____

_____

_____

Day 6

Today I mindfully regard any people who have hurt or offended me as my personal teachers. This is what I have learned from them...

_____

_____

_____

_____

_____

_____

_____

_____

_____

_____

_____

_____

_____

Day 7

Today I examine myself honestly to see how any of my words, actions, choices, or beliefs are inviting discord rather than peace. This is what I discovered about myself, and how I intend to change...

_____

_____

_____

_____

_____

_____

_____

_____

_____

_____

_____

_____

Loving-Kindness Meditation

"And how does one abide with one's hearts imbued with loving-kindness extending outward in one direction? Just as one would feel friendliness on seeing a dearly beloved friend, so does one extend loving-kindness to all creatures."

Buddha

Your interactions with other people during your day can be a challenge to mindfulness. People often say and do things that push our most sensitive buttons and stir up our insecurities. Those around us who are living unconsciously can infect us with their anger, negativity, and resentments, making it hard for us to respond thoughtfully.

One of the best ways to protect yourself from the pain of difficult interactions is through the practice of a loving-kindness meditation. The beauty of a loving-kindness meditation is that it has no conditions. It doesn't matter whether someone "deserves" it or not. Nor is it restricted to your friends and family. Rather, your loving-kindness meditation can extend from people you know to include all sentient beings.

With this practice, you begin by sitting in meditation and focusing on your breath. Then you will repeat the following phrases for specific people, as well as for you. Allow feelings of love, tenderness, and compassion to fill your heart and mind.

- *"May you be free from inner and outer harm and danger."*
- *"May you be safe and protected."*
- *"May you be free of mental suffering or distress."*
- *"May you be happy."*
- *"May you be free of physical pain and suffering."*
- *"May you be healthy and strong."*
- *"May you be able to live in this world happily, peacefully, joyfully, with ease."*

Best time to journal: *morning or evening*

Day 1

Today I practice a loving-kindness meditation for someone I love and care about deeply. This is the person, and what I experienced during the meditation...

_____

_____

_____

_____

_____

_____

_____

_____

_____

_____

_____

Day 2

Today I practice a loving-kindness meditation for a close and cherished friend. This is the person, and what I experienced during the meditation...

_____

_____

_____

_____

_____

_____

_____

_____

_____

_____

_____

_____

_____

Day 3

Today I practice a loving-kindness meditation for someone I feel neutral about. This is the person, and what I experienced during the meditation...

_____

_____

_____

_____

_____

_____

_____

_____

_____

_____

_____

_____

_____

Day 4

Today I practice a loving-kindness meditation for someone I know who has caused me pain. This is the person, and what I experienced during the meditation...

_____

_____

_____

_____

_____

_____

_____

_____

_____

_____

_____

_____

Day 5

Today I practice a loving-kindness meditation for someone who is suffering. This is the person, and what I experienced during the meditation...

_____

_____

_____

_____

_____

_____

_____

_____

_____

_____

_____

_____

Day 6

Today I practice a loving-kindness meditation for someone in the world who is causing pain or harm to others. This is the person, and what I experienced during the meditation...

_____

_____

_____

_____

_____

_____

_____

_____

_____

_____

_____

_____

Day 7

Today I practice a loving-kindness meditation for me.
This is what I experienced during the meditation...

_____

_____

_____

_____

_____

_____

_____

_____

_____

_____

_____

_____

WEEK 45

Noticing Where Attention Goes

"Where attention goes, energy flows."

James Redfield

We have spoken of mindfulness as focused attention. When you live in the present moment, your mental energy is directed to what is happening right now instead of what happened in the past or what will occur in the future.

This is one of those "hidden in plain sight" concepts that is so obvious that it's difficult to fully grasp and consistently apply. Your attention—your state of mindfulness—is a directing of energy. Where you aim your attention is what you choose to give power to.

If you choose to focus on distractions, negativity, anger, or unhappiness, your energy will be funneled into those things. If you choose to focus on the task at hand, the present moment, gratitude, or the beauty of nature, then your energy flows into these things.

Awareness and choice of where your attention goes can make the difference between a positive or negative state of mind; reaching a state of flow or being distracted; deepening your relationships or being disconnected. This week you will focus on where you want energy to flow, and choosing to direct your attention to these things.

Best time to journal: *morning*

Day 1

*Where do I want my energy to flow today? This is what I intend
to do to harness my attention to this endeavor
so that energy flows into it...*

_____

_____

_____

_____

_____

_____

_____

_____

_____

_____

Day 2

*Where do I want my energy to flow today? This is what I intend
to do to harness my attention to this endeavor
so that energy flows into it...*

_____

_____

_____

_____

_____

_____

_____

_____

_____

_____

_____

Day 3

*Where do I want my energy to flow today? This is what I intend
to do to harness my attention to this endeavor
so that energy flows into it...*

_____

_____

_____

_____

_____

_____

_____

_____

_____

_____

_____

Day 4

*Where do I want my energy to flow today? This is what I intend
to do to harness my attention to this endeavor
so that energy flows into it...*

Day 5

*Where do I want my energy to flow today? This is what I intend
to do to harness my attention to this endeavor
so that energy flows into it...*

_____

_____

_____

_____

_____

_____

_____

_____

_____

_____

_____

Day 6

*Where do I want my energy to flow today? This is what I intend
to do to harness my attention to this endeavor
so that energy flows into it...*

_____

_____

_____

_____

_____

_____

_____

_____

_____

_____

_____

_____

Day 7

*Where do I want my energy to flow today? This is what I intend
to do to harness my attention to this endeavor
so that energy flows into it...*

_____

_____

_____

_____

_____

_____

_____

_____

_____

_____

_____

WEEK 46

Take a Mental Vacation

"Change your mental imagery, and the feelings will take care of themselves."

Maxwell Maltz

As the day ends, your body and mind have accumulated stress, leaving you exhausted and mentally drained. Even on easy days, you're faced with minor decisions and aggravations that deplete you. We often carry that agitation home with us, without a peaceful transition from the demands of the day to the start of the evening.

You can create this transition by using a simple visualization practice—a mental vacation. By visualizing your perfect relaxation spot, you put yourself into a positive state so you can move on more mindfully to your evening activities.

Begin by getting into a meditative state with focused breathing. Think about a place where you feel completely happy and relaxed. You might think about sitting on a beautiful beach at sunset watching the waves, or sitting in a lush, quiet forest by a babbling stream.

Mentally immerse yourself in this peaceful spot using all of your senses. Visualize minute details, paying attention to the positive feelings the setting evokes. Then view yourself in this beautiful, soothing setting. What are you doing? Notice how calm and relaxed you look, and how happy you appear. Let a smile spread on your face as you look at yourself feeling so great.

Best time to journal: *evening*

Day 1

Today during my mental vacation meditation, this is where I went, what I noticed, and how I felt...

_____

_____

_____

_____

_____

_____

_____

_____

_____

_____

_____

_____

Day 2

Today during my mental vacation meditation, this is where I went, what I noticed, and how I felt...

_____

_____

_____

_____

_____

_____

_____

_____

_____

_____

_____

_____

Day 3

Today during my mental vacation meditation, this is where I went, what I noticed, and how I felt...

_____

_____

_____

_____

_____

_____

_____

_____

_____

_____

_____

_____

_____

Day 4

Today during my mental vacation meditation, this is where I went, what I noticed, and how I felt...

_____

_____

_____

_____

_____

_____

_____

_____

_____

_____

_____

Day 5

Today during my mental vacation meditation, this is where I went, what I noticed, and how I felt...

_____

_____

_____

_____

_____

_____

_____

_____

_____

_____

_____

Day 6

Today during my mental vacation meditation, this is where I went, what I noticed, and how I felt...

_____

_____

_____

_____

_____

_____

_____

_____

_____

_____

_____

_____

Day 7

Today during my mental vacation meditation, this is where I went, what I noticed, and how I felt...

_____

_____

_____

_____

_____

_____

_____

_____

_____

_____

_____

_____

Exploring Fear and Anxiety

"Nothing in life is to be feared, it is only to be understood. Now is the time to understand more, so that we may fear less."

Marie Curie

Fear is our mind and body's evolutionary response to perceived threats—the "fight or flight" response that kept our ancestors alert for real danger. Today, fear shows up more often as anxiety—a foreboding of possible future misfortune. Every day we hear about terrible things like accidents, illness, loss, and death. These things make us keenly aware of our own vulnerability to calamity.

Many of our fears arise from the fact that everything changes—we age, our children grow up, people leave us, and every living thing dies, including us. Fear and anxiety can often hinder our ability to function in life, so our natural reaction is to avoid fear through distraction, medication, and denial.

Mindfulness teaches us a different way to approach fear and anxiety. Rather than judging and resisting it, we approach it with compassion and curiosity, which can reduce the grip of anxiety. Allowing your fear space without resistance gives it the freedom to dissipate.

Best time to journal: *various times of day*

Day 1

Today I contemplate one of my biggest fears. I visualize it as a person
sitting across from me, and show compassion and kindness toward it.
I ask my fear, "What do I need to know about you?"
This is what my fear told me...

_____

_____

_____

_____

_____

_____

_____

_____

_____

_____

_____

Day 2

Today I return to one of my biggest fears and visualize putting it into a helium balloon. I release the balloon and watch it float away and out of sight. This is what I experienced with this exercise...

_____

_____

_____

_____

_____

_____

_____

_____

_____

_____

_____

_____

Day 3

Today I notice my fears and anxieties as they arise through the day, and pay attention to what triggers them and how they show up in me. This is what I noticed...

_____

_____

_____

_____

_____

_____

_____

_____

_____

_____

_____

_____

Day 4

I examine one of my fears using logic. I ask myself, "What is the worst that can happen?" "Can I do anything to change the thing I fear?" "Is my fear grounded in reality?" These are my answers...

_____

_____

_____

_____

_____

_____

_____

_____

_____

_____

_____

_____

Day 5

Today I write a letter to my fearful self from the perspective of my higher, wiser self. Here is my letter...

Day 6

Today I practice a short breathing meditation. I breathe in love, imagining cleansing, healing energy entering my body. I breath out fear, imagining pain and darkness leaving my body. This is what I noticed with my meditation...

_____

_____

_____

_____

_____

_____

_____

_____

_____

_____

_____

Day 7

I contemplate the truth that fear and anxiety are just feelings that arise from my thoughts. Fear itself cannot harm me. I visualize releasing fear like letting go of my grasp on a ledge. I trust life to catch me and unfold as it should. This is what I experienced...

_____

_____

_____

_____

_____

_____

_____

_____

_____

_____

_____

_____

Mindfully Review Your Day

"It is when you lose sight of yourself that you lose your way. To keep your truth in sight you must keep yourself in sight, and the world should be a mirror to reflect to you your image; the world should be a mirror that you reflect upon."

C. JoyBell C.

We often take time before a new year to review the previous year and what has been accomplished. This yearly review invites self-awareness and recalibration. An annual self-assessment is a valuable exercise when it comes to your major life goals.

This yearly review is useful, but the best way to know how you're doing in life is a check-in with how present and mindful you are on a daily basis. It's important to watch your progress, see what is working for you and what isn't, and then challenge yourself to build your "mindfulness muscle" every day.

At the end of the day, when the house is quiet and you've finished all your tasks, sit down for a few minutes of self-reflection. *How have you done with your mindfulness practices? How were they helpful or challenging? In what interactions or situations were you unconscious and mindless? Were there times when you were reactive, unfocused, or distracted? Did you have periods when your mind was racing, looping, and longing?* Write about your observations.

Best time to journal: *evening or before bed*

Day 1

I review my day to check in on my efforts (or lack of efforts) with mindfulness. The is what I noticed and where I need to improve...

Day 2

I review my day to check in on my efforts (or lack of efforts) with mindfulness. The is what I noticed and where I need to improve...

_____

_____

_____

_____

_____

_____

_____

_____

_____

_____

_____

_____

Day 3

I review my day to check in on my efforts (or lack of efforts) with mindfulness. The is what I noticed and where I need to improve...

_____

_____

_____

_____

_____

_____

_____

_____

_____

_____

_____

_____

Day 4

I review my day to check in on my efforts (or lack of efforts) with mindfulness. The is what I noticed and where I need to improve...

_____

_____

_____

_____

_____

_____

_____

_____

_____

_____

_____

_____

_____

Day 5

I review my day to check in on my efforts (or lack of efforts) with mindfulness. The is what I noticed and where I need to improve...

_____

_____

_____

_____

_____

_____

_____

_____

_____

_____

_____

_____

Day 6

I review my day to check in on my efforts (or lack of efforts) with mindfulness. The is what I noticed and where I need to improve...

_____

_____

_____

_____

_____

_____

_____

_____

_____

_____

_____

_____

Day 7

I review my day to check in on my efforts (or lack of efforts) with mindfulness. The is what I noticed and where I need to improve...

_____

_____

_____

_____

_____

_____

_____

_____

_____

_____

_____

WEEK 49

Practice a Walking Meditation

*"The mind can go in a thousand directions, but on this beautiful path,
I walk in peace. With each step, the wind blows.
With each step, a flower blooms."*

Thích Nhất Hạnh

A walking meditation is an active mindfulness habit where you are moving in the environment, rather than sitting in a chair or on a cushion on the floor. Unlike seated meditation, in which you are withdrawn into yourself, a walking meditation requires engaging all your senses. You are intentionally aware of your feet hitting the ground, the sights around you, the air you are breathing, and hearing every sound.

This is a practice that allows you to be more connected with nature, which is an essential part of who we are. A walking meditation is usually done much more slowly than normal walks, and your pace should be steady and even.

This week you will practice various walking meditations to enhance your mindfulness practices. Before you start your walking session, spend a minute or two just standing there, breathing deeply and anchoring your attention in your body. Maintain the attitude that there is nothing to achieve except mastering your attention and presence. Simply be with the process.

Best time to journal: *any time of day*

Day 1

Today I choose a straight path of about 30 to 40 feet for my walking meditation. I walk back and forth on the path, paying attention to the soles of my feet. When my mind wanders, I return focus to the soles of my feet. This is what I experienced in my meditation...

_____

_____

_____

_____

_____

_____

_____

_____

_____

_____

_____

Day 2

I choose a walking path of any length, and focus on an affirmation of my choosing for my in and out breaths (i.e., breathing in "I am here," breathing out "In the now.") I return again and again to my affirmation. This is what I experienced in my meditation...

_____

_____

_____

_____

_____

_____

_____

_____

_____

_____

_____

_____

Day 3

In my walking meditation, I am present with sounds, noticing my feet hitting the ground, the birds singing, the wind rustling the leaves. This is what I experienced in my meditation...

_____

_____

_____

_____

_____

_____

_____

_____

_____

_____

_____

Day 4

In my walking meditation, I am focused on breathing. I inhale for four steps, retain the breath for four steps, exhale slowly for four steps, and retain empty for four steps. This is what I experienced in my meditation...

_____

_____

_____

_____

_____

_____

_____

_____

_____

_____

_____

Day 5

Today in my walking meditation, I walk to an important or meaningful spot (a place in nature, my place of worship, a gravesite, etc.), focused on the feelings this place holds for me. This is what I experienced in my meditation...

_____

_____

_____

_____

_____

_____

_____

_____

_____

_____

_____

_____

_____

Day 6

Today in my walking meditation, I walk in a large circle without noticing my surroundings. I focus on a mantra that I write for myself, repeating it over and over. This is my mantra, and what I experienced in my meditation...

_____

_____

_____

_____

_____

_____

_____

_____

_____

_____

_____

Day 7

I choose the type of walking meditation that feels right for today.
This is what I experienced in my meditation...

_____

_____

_____

_____

_____

_____

_____

_____

_____

_____

_____

_____

_____

Noticing Comparison

*"A flower does not think of competing
to the flower next to it, it just blooms."*

Zen Shin

We compare ourselves to others—it's human nature. We want to know where we rank in the pecking order. We want to feel included, worthy, equal, or even superior.

Sometimes comparison motivates us to be or do better, but more often it causes suffering. We want what we don't have, and feel inferior as a result. We project our feelings about ourselves onto others by expressing resentment, jealousy, or contempt. This adds more suffering and separates us further from ourselves and others.

Comparison and mindfulness cannot coexist. Comparison robs us of the present moment and deprives us of joy. It ignites a spark of negativity in our minds that can lead to ruminating and anxiety. It pulls us away from gratitude for what we have right here, right now.

This week you will notice how you compare yourself to others, and the emotions behind your comparisons. As you shine the light of awareness on this tendency, you can mindfully bring your attention back to a more positive mindset.

Best time to journal: *morning or evening*

Day 1

Today I contemplate where and how I tend to compare myself to others.
These are the ways I compare myself...

_____

_____

_____

_____

_____

_____

_____

_____

_____

_____

_____

Day 2

Looking at my list of ways I compare myself, I consider the self-defeating thoughts and feelings that motivate my comparisons. These are the thoughts and feelings behind my comparisons...

_____

_____

_____

_____

_____

_____

_____

_____

_____

_____

_____

Day 3

*Today I choose to focus on my strengths and aptitudes rather than what
I am lacking, to see how much I have and how grateful I feel.
This is a list of my strengths and aptitudes...*

_____

_____

_____

_____

_____

_____

_____

_____

_____

_____

_____

_____

Day 4

Today I focus on the intangible treasures in life that I have access to at any time (like love, empathy, selflessness, generosity), and how I can increase these higher pursuits. These are the pursuits I choose, and how I can focus more on them...

_____

_____

_____

_____

_____

_____

_____

_____

_____

_____

_____

_____

Day 5

Today I think about outcomes I want to achieve, and shift my attention from the outcome to the process. I look for the joy in doing rather than in getting what I want. These are the ways I can find joy in the process...

_____

_____

_____

_____

_____

_____

_____

_____

_____

_____

_____

_____

Day 6

Today I think about someone I perceive as better than me or having something I want. I view them through a more realistic lens, thinking about their humanness and the frailties that all people share. I feel empathy and compassion for them rather than envy or resentment. This is what I noticed...

_____

_____

_____

_____

_____

_____

_____

_____

_____

_____

_____

_____

_____

Day 7

Today I focus on finding inspiration from those I tend to compare myself to, rather than feeling longing or jealousy. This is how they inspire me...

_____

_____

_____

_____

_____

_____

_____

_____

_____

_____

_____

_____

Mindful Fun and Play

> *"In all of living, have much fun and laughter. Life is to be enjoyed, not just endured."*

Gordon B. Hinckley

Does mindfulness sometimes feel like serious business? Especially at the beginning of a mindfulness practice, it can feel like hard work. Staying present. Noticing thoughts. Returning to your breathing over and over again. Choosing mindful ways to deal with difficult emotions. Does it always have to be so challenging?

It is true that mindfulness is a practice, and any practice requires repetition, discipline, and plenty of failures and disappointments before it becomes effortless. The ultimate goal of mindfulness is to find joy in each and every moment, but it takes cultivation to realize that goal.

In our adult lives, we struggle more than we did as children to experience pure joy in the moment. As children, our play was fully in the moment. We didn't ponder whether we were having fun. We just had fun. As we grow older, we lose the capacity for unadulterated fun. This week you will focus on giving yourself over to fun and play as you did when you were young, without judgment or analysis.

Best time to journal: *various times of day*

Day 1

Today I think about all of the things that feel like fun and play to me,
and that bring me joy without self-judgment.
These are the things...

_____

_____

_____

_____

_____

_____

_____

_____

_____

_____

_____

Day 2

*I choose one item on my list and give myself time
to enjoy it today with the mindset of a child.
This is what I did and what I experienced...*

_____

_____

_____

_____

_____

_____

_____

_____

_____

_____

_____

_____

Day 3

I choose one item on my list and give myself time
to enjoy it today with the mindset of a child.
This is what I did and what I experienced...

_____

_____

_____

_____

_____

_____

_____

_____

_____

_____

_____

Day 4

I choose one item on my list and give myself time to enjoy it today with the mindset of a child. This is what I did and what I experienced...

_____

_____

_____

_____

_____

_____

_____

_____

_____

_____

_____

_____

_____

Day 5

*I choose one item on my list and give myself time
to enjoy it today with the mindset of a child.
This is what I did and what I experienced...*

Day 6

*I choose one item on my list and give myself time
to enjoy it today with the mindset of a child.
This is what I did and what I experienced...*

_____

_____

_____

_____

_____

_____

_____

_____

_____

_____

_____

Day 7

I choose one item on my list and give myself time
to enjoy it today with the mindset of a child.
This is what I did and what I experienced...

Your Longings and Cravings

"Let not our longing slay the appetite of our living."

Jim Elliot

A big impediment to living mindfully is dealing with our discontent—longing for more money, a happier relationship, a bigger home, a better job. We long for things to be the way they used to be, or how we planned for them to be. We long for an end to pain, disappointment, suffering, and unhappiness.

We feel our longings in our gut, constantly simmering on low boil. We attach our happiness to having these longings met. Our cravings are more visceral. They are the daily itches that must be scratched. We crave our coffee in the morning to wake up, a cocktail in the evening to wind down, or a quick fix from our smartphones.

The more we give in to our longings and cravings, the more power they have over us. They keep us agitated, anxious, and frustrated. When our desires aren't fulfilled, when we can't have what we want, we loop our disappointments over and over in our minds, which intensifies our unhappy feelings. When you become so attached to what you don't have, you have no availability for the beautiful reality in front of you.

Best time to journal: *morning or evening*

Day 1

Today I notice any feelings of frustration, agitation, anxiety, disappointment, or anger that are tied to my longing for something I don't have. What do I notice, and what are the longings?

_____

_____

_____

_____

_____

_____

_____

_____

_____

_____

_____

Day 2

As I become aware of my longings, I ask myself, "In what ways do I feel unfulfilled that creates this longing in me?"

_____

_____

_____

_____

_____

_____

_____

_____

_____

_____

_____

Day 3

Today I practice a meditation where I visualize my longing as a cloud floating through my mind. I recognize that my longing is only a thought that has no power over me. I let the cloud float out of my consciousness. This is what I noticed in meditation...

Day 4

Today I focus on gratitude, and ask myself, "How is my life complete right here and now?" This is what came up for me...

_____

_____

_____

_____

_____

_____

_____

_____

_____

_____

_____

Day 5

Today I pay attention to the various cravings I have during the day
(for food, cigarettes, alcohol, checking social media, etc.).
These are the things I find myself craving...

Day 6

Today, when I notice a craving arise, I intentionally wait 10 minutes without giving in to the craving. What did I notice about my craving when I didn't give in to it right away?

_____

_____

_____

_____

_____

_____

_____

_____

_____

_____

_____

Day 7

Today I make a mindful choice about one of my cravings to choose something different and better for me. I see I have power over my craving. This is what I experienced...

Final Thoughts...

Congratulations on completing *The Mindfulness Journal.*

We encourage you to read back through your writing to see how you have grown in mindful awareness over the last 52 weeks, and pinpoint ways you can deepen your practice going forward. Like any skill, mindfulness requires regular repetition before it becomes natural.

In fact, we recommend turning any mindfulness practices that you particularly enjoyed into daily habits. For instance, if you felt more peaceful and centered after a few minutes of walking meditation, then make sure that you carve out time every day to enjoy the sights and sounds of nature.

Hopefully you will find a way to make mindfulness a part of every day, even if it is just by being more attentive to the task at hand or taking a few minutes for mindful breathing.

Also, remember to become the "watcher" of your thoughts when they are negative or troubling, rather than allowing your thoughts to determine your state of mind. Do your best to savor as many "right nows" as possible — because right now is really all you have.

We would love to hear about your experiences with these mindfulness practices, and which ones you found most useful. Please connect with us on our Facebook fan page at themindfulnesslife.com and share your thoughts.

Warmly,

Barrie Davenport
S.J. Scott

Our *Gift* to You

We've covered a wealth of mindfulness practices in this journal, but that doesn't mean your self-educational efforts should end here. In fact, we've created a mindfulness companion course that includes a variety of support resources.

Here are just a few things we've included:

- The 13-step quick start checklist to quickly identify useful mindfulness habits .

- A list of useful books on mindfulness.

- A 30-day gratitude worksheet in a downloadable PDF file.

- An extensive list of positive affirmations in a downloadable PDF file.

- Mindfulness questions for couples in a downloadable PDF file.

- A video walkthrough of the mindfulness and meditation Headspace app.

- A list of 155 ways to reward yourself for accomplishing a goal or task.

Plus, we will be adding more goodies to this website in the months to come. So, if you're interested in expanding on what you've learned with this journal, then go to this page to access the course:

mindfulz.com

Thank you!

Finally, thank you for investing both your time and money in
The Mindfulness Journal.

We hope you enjoyed this journey of discovering different ways to apply
mindfulness to your daily life. You could have picked from dozens of
journals, but you took a chance and checked out this one.

Now we'd like to ask for a small favor.
**Could you please take a minute or two and leave
a review for this journal on Amazon?**

Here's the link:

http://www.DevelopGoodHabits.com/TMJ

This feedback will help us continue to write the kind of books and journals
that help you get results. And if you loved it, please let us know.

Made in the USA
San Bernardino, CA
20 July 2018